The Fourth Republic

A Possible Future for the Uganda Nation

A personal View by:

Emmanuel Sunlight Kirunda

authorHOUSE®

AuthorHouse™
1663 Liberty Drive
Bloomington, IN 47403
www.authorhouse.com
Phone: 1-800-839-8640

First published by AuthorHouse 2/23/2011

ISBN: 978-1-4567-3780-1 (sc)
ISBN: 978-1-4567-3781-8 (e)

Library of Congress Control Number: 2011902139

Printed in the United States of America

Any people depicted in stock imagery provided by Thinkstock are models,
and such images are being used for illustrative purposes only.
Certain stock imagery © Thinkstock.

This book is printed on acid-free paper.

Because of the dynamic nature of the Internet, any web addresses or
links contained in this book may have changed since publication and
may no longer be valid. The views expressed in this work are solely those
of the author and do not necessarily reflect the views of the publisher,
and the publisher hereby disclaims any responsibility for them.

Other books by the same author

Book 1: The Fourth Heritage

DEDICATION

To those Ugandan boys and girls who are dreaming and imagining things they have no means to express.

****

I prefer the dreams of the future more than the history of the past

- *Thomas Jefferson*
(Author of the American Declaration of Independence)

****

Knowledge will forever govern ignorance; and a people who mean to be their own governors must arm themselves with the power which knowledge gives.

- *James Madison*
(Author of the American Constitution)

Uganda Coat of Arms

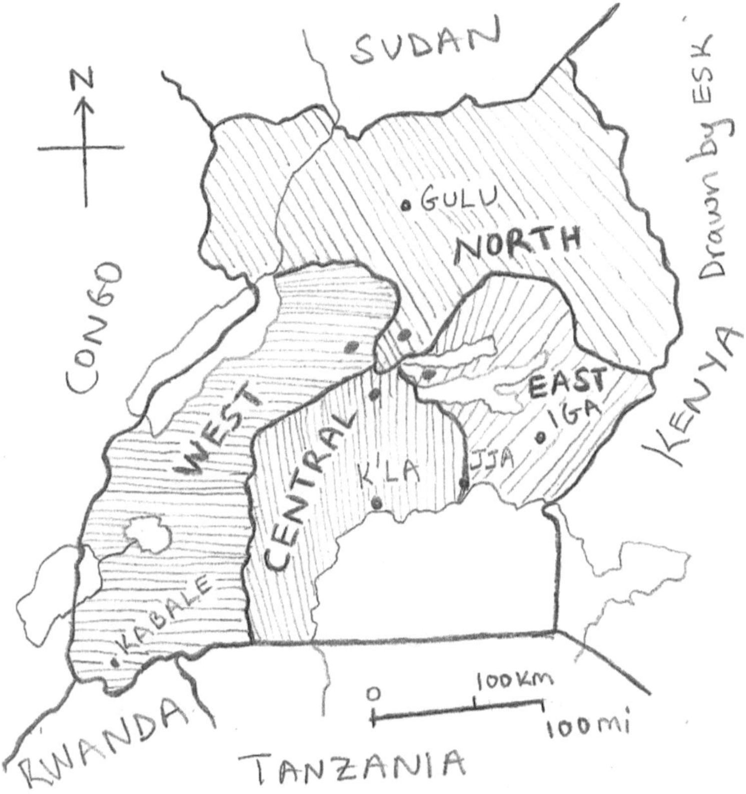

Map of Uganda

CONTENTS

FIGURES

FOREWORD

"Progress is impossible without change, and those who cannot change their minds cannot change anything."
~George Bernard Shaw~

I am a Ugandan citizen who like the author Kirunda, has had the privilege to live and study both inside and outside Uganda. Our paths first crossed at Kings College Budo in Uganda and like the author, I was offered the scholarship to represent Uganda at the United World Colleges. Our paths crossed once again in Chicago at the 2009 Ugandan North American Association Convention as Kirunda embarked on a tour to promote his first book *The Fourth Heritage*. The first book offers a strong foundation for *The Fourth Republic* and I recommend reading *The Fourth Heritage* in order to fully grasp and appreciate the concepts introduced in *The Fourth Republic*.

When I first set foot on foreign soil in the developed world, I marveled at the technology, efficiency and quality of social services, high standard of living, cleanliness, elegance, system of governance and punctuality, among others. I kept asking rhetorically, why can't we do this? Uganda has been stuck in a cycle of political and social turmoil like many other African nations in the post-colonial era. The leadership establishment has failed to free our society from the heavy burden of cultural, tribal and religious complexities. *The Fourth Republic* by Kirunda stands out as one of the most original works rendered towards lifting the weight of tribalism and groupthink off the shoulders of a static and stagnant society.

Questions have lingered for generations and the lack of solutions has been manifested by the political and social chaos in Uganda. How can we overcome our ethnic and tribal differences and co-exist as a nation? How can we harness the similarities among our cultures and tribal origins? How can we emerge from the shadows of our colonial masters and re-define our identity? How can we instill the virtues of knowledge and information in our society? How can we integrate our tribal heritage and modern systems of governance into a cohesive functional nation-state? How can we clip the wings of tribalism and groupthink to liberate our minds?

Kirunda answers these questions and offers a sweeping viewpoint by creating a well thought out "Chwezi nation." *The Fourth Republic* is an extraordinary book with a detailed roadmap that if followed and implemented can procure Ugandans a more effective system of governance. The propositions offer each Ugandan citizen the 'Chwezi dream.' This dream has a foundation rooted in clearing the path for prosperity for each individual, shaped by the promises of their imagination. The "Chwezi dream", promises to liberate Ugandans from the shackles of tribalism, poverty, ignorance, religious divisiveness and cultural conflicts. My hope is for this message to reach every Ugandan and African particularly those leading or aspiring to lead our nations in the coming years.

Dr. Kawuma Daniel
Pharm. D
West Virginia (U.S.A), November 2010

Author's Note

We have many experts—engineers, doctors, and other professionals who are mere tools. They can be used to make weapons to kill people, or they can be used to manufacture chemicals for the good of society... You, as young people, should be at the forefront of making sacrifices for Africa... Your mission is to understand the politics of your country, and Africa in general, in order to discover negative and positive politics. You must discover the path Africa should take in order to get out of the situation in which we find ourselves. Whatever profession you choose, you should be an instrument in the struggle for the greater understanding of the economic, social, and political problems of Africa. (Museveni, pg.145)

I am proud and happy to be a citizen of the country they called Uganda. Because citizenship comes with civic duties, I have taken it as my duty to suggest specific propositions that I believe can better our Country. Since childhood, I have always had an inclination towards spatial knowledge (as opposed to literary linguistic knowledge), and this book is not a historical or political narrative but rather it takes on the general framework of a visual model arranged in space and time. I once read that one of the prerequisites of becoming Prime Minister in China in the 5th century B.C. was that you had to construct a model state in your home district. Supposedly, the biggest life regret for the greatest Chinese of all time, Confucius, was that he never got a chance to try building a model state in his mind or in his district. I have created this model, not as a service or sacrifice but rather as a civic duty to contribute something to our national discourse. And I don't expect any special reward or treatment; the act of creating the ideas and concepts in this book is satisfying enough.

This book is a continuation of my previous book *The Fourth Heritage*, in which I discussed how each individual Ugandan could integrate our triple heritages of Tribe, Religion and Colonial heritages. Under the guidance of my imperfect human mind, I have created the ideas, models and concepts in both books. This work is far from perfect, but I believe it can contribute a few original ideas to the much-needed personal and societal development that we must embark on. That being said, I think I will spend my entire lifetime, wherever I may reside, trying to convince and persuade the leaders in our Country about these ideas. Unfortunately, if I fail in my persuasion, I will have no choice but to live—just like any other law-abiding citizen—according to the laws and systems that our leaders put in place. It is my strongest belief that unlike the past when people had to get guns and fight for our liberation, the new paradigm advocated for in this book involves people fighting for our liberation by writing books and working in libraries across every village and town. For God and my country!

Introduction

This brings me to my first point, which is about the consciousness of young people in Africa, the consciousness of the elite. As young people in the University, your role is to ensure that you discover what is wrong with Africa... Africa is in its present situation because of previous phenomena, which we must understand... I am not impressed that somebody is an engineer or a doctor if he does not want to know anything about politics. (Museveni, pg. 144)

According to the United Nations, Uganda is one of the 192 countries in the world. Just like other countries, Uganda is referred to as a nation-state or a republic. At the end of the colonial era, Uganda became a sovereign nation on October 9th, 1962 by attaining independence from Britain. This initial sovereign nation was a parliamentary republic with the King of Buganda as the head of state and Dr. Apollo Milton Obote as the executive Prime

Minister. That republic collapsed to yield the second republic, a presidential republic, in 1966. The new constitution of 1995 ushered in a third republic, which is also a presidential republic. This model proposes a new consensus-building paradigm for a fourth republic with particularly two objectives. 1) To bring about a strong nationalism –independent of politics –for every generation of Ugandans. This nationalism is intended to supersede the two prevailing emotional attachments that people have, namely, tribal and religious emotional attachments. 2) However, since nationalism is not always good – many bad and cruel periods in our human history have been brought about by nationalism—, the national model presented herein also aims to build an open society in which the citizenry can adopt non-Ugandan knowledge and fully welcome non-Ugandans as rightful citizens (if they choose to become citizens), because of the common humanity among all human beings on this planet. In pursuing these objectives, we should rely on championing the "self-evident truth" that as countrymen and women we have the right and liberty to envision a new national paradigm, using any and all imaginations accessible to us as thinking creatures.

The Webster dictionary defines a paradigm as *a philosophical and theoretical framework of a scientific school or discipline within which theories, laws, and generalizations and the experiments performed in support of them are formulated.* However, the word is also commonly used to refer to a particular frame of reference for human affairs. For example, one can rightfully say that Ugandans are operating in the British Colonial paradigm because we have British system of laws, we use the British language in all national affairs, our education system is based on the British system of education, etc. Still, another person could say that we are operating under a tribal-identity paradigm because an overwhelming majority of Ugandans identify first with their tribes at the expense of national progress. Since we are living in a world of nation-states, I believe Ugandans should come together and agree on a national paradigm that transcends the colonial heritage, tribal affinities and religious dogmas.

The Fourth Republic suggests a paradigm shift in nationhood; one founded on the social cohesion of society, effectiveness of governance and tolerance of ideas and people different from oneself. The audience is meant to be any person of Ugandan citizenship. The simplicity in my writing is meant to facilitate easy comprehension of the subject matter when translated into our different indigenous languages since most of our people are not literate and can't understand complex English. This book invites you as a Ugandan to realize that you can and should feel courageous to think and propose how our society should be organized.

As with any true human endeavor, this model was inspired not by a divine stimulus or supernatural powers but rather by a subjective motive to see my country prosper. However, I hope that objectivity transpires in my writing so that you the reader can embrace the propositions that I am setting forth. Where the reader senses subjective biases, it should be your duty to suggest objective improvements in the form of constructive critiques or better versions of this model. Towards this end, you can contact me at *www.4thheritage.com*

The substance of this book does not deal with analysis, blaming, or criticism of the numerous obstacles and problems in the country, but rather it sets out to propose specific arguable ideas that could be agreed upon to create a strong nation. Since the ability to analyze and then create are the two mental functions that differentiate humans from all other species, I did the very human thing and analyzed our Ugandan human condition in my first book *The Fourth Heritage* and in this follow-up book, I am doing another very human activity of creating words, concepts and institutions. I believe that failure on my part to engage in these two cerebral functions (analysis and creation) would have meant that I was living my human life below the God-given evolutionary potential.

In the beginning, the area called Uganda was not inhabited by any of us present Ugandans, except for the few pygmies (the Batwa and Bambuti). We all migrated to the area hundreds or thousands of years ago. Since the oral tradition characteristic of most of the Ugandan peoples has a very wide range of uncertainty, we cannot specifically pinpoint when and how we actually migrated to the area. But we know that for the majority tribal grouping (the Bantu), we have our origin in the Niger-Congo Delta area of West Africa while the Luo tribes have their origins in the Sudan. Our tribal myths and legendary accounts of each tribe's origin and spiritualism has come under serious strain as they have been debunked by modern scientific knowledge and almost made extinct by more powerful religious doctrines. This reality has left most of us conflicted culturally and psychologically. In their book *Peoples and Cultures of Uganda*, Nzita and Niwampa write that four major groups of peoples (Bantu, Luo, Atekerin and Sudanic groups) migrated to the present-day Uganda and assimilated or displaced the indigenous peoples to the point that these four tribal groups presently make up more than 99.9% of the population of the country. In our new home, we immigrants dispersed and adapted different customs, traditions and languages such that at the present time, Ugandans belong to distinct tribes that were a single group at one point down the road of history.

There is no doubt that hundreds of years ago, the Basoga, Bakiga, Baganda, Banyankole, Banyoro, Bagisu, Batoro, Banyarwanda, to mention just a few, were one people speaking one language. To underscore the similarity between the languages spoken by dozens of tribes in Uganda and other parts of Africa, words like "omukazi", " omwana" or " omugole" have similar meanings in many tribal languages in Uganda, Central, East and Southern Africa. Another example that shows our close similarity is the fact that in Lusoga siblings are called "abaganda" which is the name of the Baganda tribe. In short, if you go back in time, just a couple of centuries ago, most of our tribes were one people. That realization should make all of us become civilized by evolving so that we embrace the common ancestry that should unite us, instead of dwelling on tribal differences.

Present Uganda is a nation-state formed between 1890 and 1926 (Nzita and Niwampa, 1) when the British East African Company declared the land largely occupied by the Buganda Kingdom as a British Protectorate. Supposedly, the area acquired its name Uganda from Arab/

Swahili mispronunciation of 'Buganda' as 'Wuganda' and the further British mispronunciation of 'wuganda' as 'Uganda'. Even if the British people did not settle in the country the way they did in Kenya, Zimbabwe and South Africa, they used a policy of indirect rule by using the Buganda Kingdom to expand and bring neighboring tribes under colonial rule. Today, Uganda stands more as a political state than a national state, because there is no national culture or identity that is stronger than the tribal cultures and identities. For example, a tribe like the Baganda might be more organized and more of a nation than the country of Uganda is a nation. Historically, the Bunyoro-Kitala Empire was more of a nation than Uganda is today. How do we build a nation that is stronger than the loose political unit that the colonialists left behind? To illustrate this predicament, Ugandans share culture, language, food, religion, tradition, identity, customs etc on a tribal basis, not on a national basis. Even if it is not a prerequisite to have one common aspect in order to be a nation, it is imperative that a nation should have a "set of things" agreed upon or ascribed to by majority of the citizenry. And the "set of things" has to be of an indigenous origin in order to be viable pillars that attract people's emotional attachment. Therefore, this model intends to identify and propose a "set of things" that can build the most consensus among the citizens of Uganda so that people from different tribes or cultural and religious groups can rise above their limiting self-sabotaging identities to come together as equal and rightful citizens of the nation.

The logic of this creative model is to use objective knowledge to interpret and create a national paradigm out of the heritages of the people who are settled in present Uganda. It is imperative that people acquire a renewed identity (see the book *The Fourth Heritage*) that will invigorate them to embrace a work ethic that leads to economic productivity in the country.

Ugandan peoples and political evolution have been the guiding realities used in structuring the institutions and divisions in this book. There is no Ugandan culture per se, but as cultures are like people—they are conceived, they grow and they die—I hope that all the tribes of

Uganda can work together so that we grow a national culture. The implementation of this model is meant to be a self-correcting process; fellow Ugandans should be able to add to and perfect this new model however way you might see fit. The model is meant to be immune to manipulations and sustained by rigorous debates and constructive criticism. Henceforth, to be accepted, the ideas herein must survive the most rigorous standards of public scrutiny and analysis. Little time has been spent writing about descriptions/definitions and more about the real form of things—form is supposed to have universal characteristics while descriptions are immanent.

Any Ugandan is free to adopt this work as theirs and use any method of initiative or creativity to advance our issues. You can own this model by understanding it according to your personal philosophies and writing a better version, e.g. I understand this model from my Fourth Heritage philosophy. No one may agree with this model unless they intimately use their full imagination to think of how Uganda can be one of the greatest countries in CULTURE and DEVELOPMENT. There is very high probability of success for this model and all Ugandans should use the leverage given herein to struggle *For God and My Country.*

Kirunda, Emmanuel Sunlight

Austin (TX) U.S.A

July 31, 2009.

Chapter I: The Assumptions

Article 1. General Provisions

There are so many things I see going wrong in many spheres of our country, Uganda. I believe the current composition and set up of our nation-state is failing to solve these problems and also failing to offer most of our Children the opportunities needed to be the best they can be. I am proposing that given the status quo, we should embark on a national reform agenda of recreating our republic. An agenda founded on our unique history and harmonious diversity. Unfortunately, I think that there are several conditions under which such a new republic can prove impossible to build. The following are the assumptions that can make the achievement of the proposed new national paradigm untenable.

ARTICLE 2. THE 10 IFS

1. If each individual is not willing to go beyond our triple heritages of tribe, religion and colonial legacy to embrace a personal fourth heritage.

2. If society does not honor and respect each individual's human right to think freely.

3. If we lack confidence in ourselves: if we do not have trust and belief in ourselves that we can rightfully set an original agenda for our destiny. An agenda that encompasses all facets of our lives. In other words, if citizens still believe in the misguided concept that only ideas and things emanating from non-Ugandans have a supposedly superior quality and mandate to them.

4. If we are not willing to give all imaginable

tools to our young children so that whether they remain within the country or they go anywhere in this world, they feel empowered and ready to work tenaciously for their individual progress.

5. If some citizens have a passion to negatively discriminate against other human beings because of biological, cultural or political differences.

6. If people are not willing to embrace an efficient work ethic that can enable them to do the hard, but fulfilling work needed for economical progress. Or, if people erroneously think that wealth lies beneath the ground instead of realizing that true wealth lies in each person's brain.

7. If people are still slaves to the past, instead of taking responsibility for the present to work tirelessly for a better future. Or, if people have blind faith that history consisted only of heroic acts by great people who arranged

things for long spans of time. That is, if people fail to embrace the fact that history is made by you and me coming up with new ideas and creations in the present time.

8. If the citizenry does not believe that each one of us has an eternal duty to propagate the process of creation that has been unfolding for the past 14 billion years.

9. If people don't want to use the explanations of natural science to shade light on cultural and religious experiences.

10. If people fail to cherish the two major brain functions that are common to all Ugandans and all non-Ugandans: the functions of analyzing and creating. In other words, if people fail to realize that limitless imagination and infinite curiosity are the driving forces behind human civilization.

Chapter II: Fundamental Pillars For Our Society

The writers of these papers-and the political pressure groups they represent- do not appear to have any idea of the direction our country should be taking... They ought to be asking: what is the cause of all our problems? What is the basis of all things that happen in life? Does life develop accidently or are there basic laws that govern the dynamics of society? (Museveni, pg. 161)

Article 3. General Provisions

In order to bring about social change necessary for a great nation-building enterprise, I believe that there are fundamental pillars, which we have to first-of-all agree upon. It is very possible to look for all encompassing fundamentals, but for brevity, it is more practical to look for as few of them as possible. The following list can enable our diverse citizenry to agree without being disagreeable

5

about the foundation of our nation-state. I think these five pillars, once agreed upon, can act as the undisputed cornerstone for social change and nation building.

ARTICLE 4. PILLAR 1-THE FOURTH HERITAGE

(1)   Ugandans come in all kinds of cultural heritages. However, according to Ali Mazrui's assessment in his book *The Africans*, we have three broad heritages: indigenous, Semitic or Judeo-Christian-Islamic, and Western/European.

(2)   As outlined in my book *The Fourth Heritage*, each individual Ugandan should strive to transcend the limits of each of our triple heritages and embrace a personal fourth heritage: "Use human skeptical reasoning to guide your embrace of a tribal identity, to understand your religious faith, and to choose the good while discarding the bad within the European colonial legacy".

ARTICLE 5. PILLAR 2 - GOD

(1)   Our National motto **For God and My Country** is the first undisputable consensus-building pillar that all Ugandans seem to agree about. There seems to be universal agreement among Ugandans that God is a fundamental entity in our lives and country. However, you need to define terms before you can talk about them. Hence, what is God that we all seem to agree about? Even before outsiders told us about Allah or Jesus or Yahweh etc, we knew God as Kibumba, Katonda, Ruhanga, Jok etc. Our peoples acknowledged the reality of a higher power or deity even before foreigners told us its/her/his specific name. There is no evidence that before foreigners came to Uganda, our ancestors understood God as a male or female entity. I believe they acknowledged Nature's God, interpreted as the Laws of Nature, which they could not understand. There is no changing history of God: What God did 10,000 year ago, God does today and God did 14 Billion years ago. At the present time, our people who don't practice Christianity or Islam have a full

7

understanding of the reality of a higher power or deity. Our republic should respect and protect those people's beliefs. I would call such people God'ists because they universally believe in God. Our motto says "For God and My Country" not "For God and Our Country". I interpret "my" to mean that the framers of our motto wanted each of us to exercise individual choice in all matters of our lives including God and Country. "Our Country" would have meant a communal interpretation of God and Country. Further more, the republic should also respect and protect the minority people that don't share the majority's belief in God. Just as a parent does not abandon his/her child however much that child rebels against the parent, why should God abandon any human being based on his/her belief?

(2)   I have never read any account, which says that before outsiders came to Uganda, we had any wars or disputes about God. The Basoga have never had any problem, let alone any war, with the Bakiga just because we knew God as Kibumba and the Bakiga knew God as

Ruhanga. Even when the Arabs told us that they knew God as Allah or the Christians knew God as Jesus, there should not have been any problem, contradictions or wars. Unfortunately, just within the Christian understanding of God, we had the most barbaric wars between the Catholics and the Protestants that eventually led to the Uganda martyrs. From my personal view, any problem that came about because of God was not about God's essence per se but rather it came about because of the imperfect human cultural traditions of relating to or understanding God. And particularly for the case of the Catholic-Protestant wars, it was mainly because of politics. Therefore, in our Fourth Republic politics, there should be no room for divisive traditions relating to God. What happened when the Arabs and Europeans brought their traditions of God was not introduction of new Gods but rather a mere paradigm shift in how we understood God. Whereas before they came, we used to give general attributes to God, after our contact with the outsiders we started giving specific attributes to God. For example, instead of our general belief that God created us, we started specifically saying that God created us on the sixth day. That God paradigm shift did not negate our prior belief in God, but rather it just refined and structured our understanding of God. And since structured systems are more durable than primitive systems (in fact most people define civilization as the building of structures), it does not take a rocket scientist to realize that it is because of the outsiders' well-structured traditions that our "primitive" traditions were vanquished. But the question now is; can we construct a more formidable national structure that can withstand and repel any future colonialist adventures?

(3)   Notwithstanding our inability to agree 100% on all the attributes of God, most people seem to believe in God's essence. Henceforth, it might be fair to say that God must have watched over our ancestors as they migrated thousands of years ago from their cradle lands to their new home, the present land of Uganda.

(4)   It is also very obvious that beyond just asserting to the concept of God, we cannot (and there is no indication

anywhere in history that people do) agree on the exact specifics of God. To save us persecutions, discrimination, bloodshed and the potential misfortunes that could befall our peoples if we go far and beyond to sanction one particular tradition of relating to God—case in mind are the Catholic Protestant wars of Kabaka Mwanga's era—the state should just stop at acknowledgement of God. People have the liberty and freedom to ascribe to particular traditions and practices concerning God. There is no way the state should come in favor of one religious tradition over the others.

(5)   I believe that God's eternal reality provides innate value and dignity to each child at birth, and despite all our inherent imperfections, our individual uniqueness and relation with God are matters solely between God and each individual. Besides giving instructive advice, no other person, be it priest or elder, has to control or dictate how individuals understand God.

ARTICLE 6. PILLAR 3 - COUNTRY

(1)   Since foreigners randomly demarcated the African continent into spheres of influence and exploitation, the present state of Uganda still resembles the entity that outsiders created for their own selfish reasons and based on their interpretation of our realities. With this new national model, we should work with our neighboring countries to see if arbitrary borders left by the colonialists need to be adjusted. There is rightful indignation that many aspects of the present nation-state don't serve the purpose of unifying all the peoples and address our aspirations as a people. Since independence, we have tried to govern ourselves first under a parliamentary federal republic, then under Obote's presidential republic model and now under NRM presidential republic model but there is still much work left to achieve a more perfect nation. The country has grown in absolute terms but as the population grows exponentially (according to the World Watch Institute, Uganda's population growth of 3.1 % is more than double the world's rate of 1.2% and the population is projected to

explode from its current 28 million people to 150 million people by 2050), the net economic growth now is less than what we had in the 1960s. It then seems logical that we need to keep working at perfecting our nationhood. This book is my personal contribution to the task of perfecting our nation.

(2)   The Constitution of the country should be looked at as a general framework for the country, to which all specific laws conform. Officially it should be called "The General Law" so that all tribal people can refer to it in their local languages since there is no tribal word for "constitution" yet all tribes have words for "general law". This general framework should be simple, very short in length (hopefully not more than 50 pages) and accessible to all citizens by way of it being written in broad terms that can be translated in all our tribal languages. The General Law (Constitution) should be written in simple English (with no complicated Latin words), so that it can easily be translated into all our tribal languages. This way, people don't have to have an education in law to

understand their natural rights, which the constitution stipulates out for them. I believe this would be in the spirit of Einstein's proposition: "things should be made as simple as possible, but not simpler". It is only specific laws made by acts of Parliament that should be written in complicated legal lingual because they are to be administered and interpreted by educated lawyers. In my view, if we have a constitution that is a complex voluminous work of laws, then the majority of the citizenry (who are illiterate) will be unfortunately dependant on the minority elite to understand their basic human rights. The country's constitution is to be the supreme law of the land, which spells out the structures and responsibilities of the branches of our national government (*see next chapter*). Any residual power not outlined in the constitution is to be exercised by the people through their representatives or their own mobilization. Any constitutional change has to be initiated by one person who has to get a minimum number of signatures before the country accepts or rejects the change via a Republic Vote (*see definition in Glossary*)

(3)   We should look into getting an original name for the country, one that is neutral and has more potential to bring about nationalism and patriotism. The agreed upon name should either refer to our endowment of natural resources or to the indigenous people who inhabited the area before we migrated here. In this book, I am proposing the name of the legendary Chwezi dynasty whose people – the Bachwezi— are talked about in many oral traditions throughout Uganda, Rwanda, Burundi, Congo, Tanzania and Western Kenya. For example my tribe still calls spiritual leaders 'baswezi', and I have read many other tribes have tales of their ancestors being 'bachwezi'. From the legend of the Bachwezi, we can find eternal connection with our prehistoric past by coming up with an original name for the country, e.g. 'The Chwezi Nation' or 'Chwezia'. For this book I use the name Chwezia, but I hope that upon public debate, we can settle on a consensus name. At first I had chosen another name 'Nilonda' derived from one of the great natural features of the country, the Nile. If we choose Chwezia, we can even decide on

the name of the nationality, in both English and tribal languages, to be Bachwezia or simply Chwezians. Similar to how there are ancient Egyptians and modern Egyptians or ancient Israelites and modern Israelis, we can see our heritage divided between the ancient Bachwezi and the modern Bachwezia. This would be a strong illustration to our future children that we took charge of our destiny by getting to the core of reconnecting our present aspirations with our pre-historical heritage.

(4)   Let national authority be divided into four branches: two political branches (the Legislature and the Executive) whose composition is based on individuals competing with other individuals for votes, and two non-political branches (Human Heritage branch and the Judiciary) whose composition is based on individuals distinguishing themselves in intellectual accomplishments. Also, country local government administration should be in two levels: Local Council divisions (Villages, Towns, Municipalities or Cities) and District Administrations (either the original 19 districts or up to 36 districts). The simple two-tier

system is meant to prevent too much governmental bureaucracies that end up being too complicated for many citizens to navigate in search of public services. The national capital should be spread among the four non-administrative regions of the country. The central region should be the seat for the Human Heritage branch. The Executive, Legislative and Judiciary seats should be spread among the three remaining regions (east, west and north).

(5)　　Let the country emblem remain: 1) **The Coat of Arms** (*See the book's front pages for the picture*) with its majestic symbols that include our national bird (the Crested Crane), the Kob, which represents our wildlife, and our national motto, "For God and My Country". 2) **National Anthem** (*See Schedules at the back*), let the first stanza be called the red stanza because it talks about human togetherness, let the second stanza be called the blue stanza because it talks about peace with our neighbors, and let the last stanza be called the yellow stanza because it talks about the sun and nature. One stanza should always be sung on ordinary occasions, two stanzas should be sung when a member of the political branches of state is in attendance and three stanzas should be sung when a member of the non-political branches of state is in attendance. If we agree to create a Fourth Republic, the national anthem should be sung with one hand crossed on the heart with four fingers stretched out. All pupils and students in the country should be familiar with the Uganda School Anthem (*See Schedules at the back for the words to the anthem*) 3) **Flag**, because of the evolution of the Uganda flag (*see appendix*), we can further continue on this process by slightly changing the flag colors to match our national anthem, i.e. by replacing black with blue. From top to bottom, the colors would then be Red, Blue and Yellow instead of Black, Yellow, Red. The top color 'red' signifies people which the first anthem stanza talks about, the middle color 'blue' signifies peace which the second stanza talks about, and the lower color 'yellow' signifies the sun, which the third stanza talks about. However, for better aesthetics and to keep the present middle color, the colors could be rearranged into

Red, Yellow and Blue because yellow givens a natural contrast between the Red and Blue. Or yellow could be replaced by green since green largely signifies nature and the sun is part of nature. The rainbow flag (the double-colored flag) should have either the Crested Crane or the Kob.

(6)   The state duty should be to recognize and cherish humanity in each individual and protect the inalienable right of each person to determine his or her life—the perfection of one's own fourth heritage is a good guide—constrained only by submission to the Law of the land to prevent anarchy.

ARTICLE 7. PILLAR 4 – ANARCHY AND TYRANNY

There shouldn't be anarchy or tyranny in the country if our national civic and political leaders agree upon and implement a more inclusive and original republican paradigm. We should ingeniously recreate our republic so that the country breaks free from its violent history and the constant fear of the next war by ensuring that we build a nation where the opposition and other people who don't support the government feel an equal share of nationhood. By recreating our republic in an original way that prevents anarchy and tyranny, our children and our children's children will never feel that they are victims of colonialism in any way, shape or form.

ARTICLE 8. PILLAR 5 - LANGUAGES

(1)   Languages don't belong to people; they are just a way to communicate understanding of the world around us. Languages evolve, for example, 1000 years ago, Latin was the most important and most powerful language in Europe, every person who wanted to access power or knowledge had to speak Latin. But now, it is almost extinct. Presently, English is the most important and most powerful language in the country and also in the world. Every person who wants to access power and knowledge in Uganda speaks and writes in English. In 1000 years

from now, English might be extinct. Let the government maintain English as the official language at the national and district levels in order to unify the country, enable the people to have access to the most robust knowledge, and also to ensure economic development. However, other East African official languages (Kiswahili, and French,) should be funded and offered to people as possible useful alternative languages. We should decide on whether to use American English or British English or come up with our own version of the English language. If we decide to come up with our own version, the Chwezi Librarian *(see Article 31 for role description)* should be the office charged with keeping and updating our Chwezi English Dictionary. The Chwezi Librarian is also charged with keeping and updating a single dictionary with words from all our tribal languages instead of the current system where individual tribes are writing their individual dictionaries.

(2)   Because of the richness of the English language, which can allow people to grasp many concepts and ideas beyond our indigenous languages (e.g. modern scientific

discoveries), all the leaders of our government and society do speak, read and write in English. Government should facilitate the process of creating words in our indigenous languages that are equivalent to English words or make sure that every citizen can speak English so that they can individually acquire knowledge and ideas beyond the tribal languages. For example, since a Musoga has the same word for country, continent, earth and universe and there are no equivalent tribal words to English phrases like 'the universe is finite but unbounded', that person's understanding of the physical world is very limited. Also, since non-schooled minds cannot understand fundamental scientific laws like Newton's law of gravity, which explains the shape and structure of planetary systems within our universe, many of them feel powerless or hopeless when told about simple ideas like "the earth is round and it revolves around the sun". Furthermore, since no indigenous language has equivalents to words like *Zeitgeist* (even English did not have this word, it was borrowed from German) or *collective unconsciousness*, it is hard for an indigenous person to fully analyze the foreign religions that now dominate our society because the analysis of placing current religious ideas in their rightful evolutionary stage is foreign to Indigenous people. Hence many of our people superstitiously embrace foreign religions they don't fully understand. The English language greatly aids in people's understanding and analysis of such important facets of people's lives.

(3)   I strongly believe English is a tool to acquire knowledge that you cannot access if you only speak your tribal language. Presently, all the leaders in the country speak English and that gives them power over the multitude of people in the villages who don't speak English. This is because English is the present universal language that allows people to do business and have cultural exchanges with other people from any part of the world. As long as we don't forsake our indigenous languages, speaking English only makes us have more options of acquiring knowledge, and with it comes power. Just as 1000 years ago in Europe, all knowledge was in Latin and every German or Frenchman had to learn Latin in order to

access immense knowledge, presently, English is the language that enables people to acquire the most up-to-date knowledge from around the world. The most up-to-date knowledge in Computer Science, Physics, Chemistry and Biology (the knowledge areas that are separating the first world from the left-behind world) are written in the English language as opposed to our tribal languages.

(4)   People who can speak English have both the intellectual power—because they know more— and the economic power because they can travel around the world and do business with anyone in the world. The following are examples that show you how speaking English can enlighten you more than if you just spoke only your tribal language. You cannot say these statements in tribal languages, yet knowing the simple concepts contained in these sentences enlightens you as a human being. 1) The Earth is not the whole universe, 2) The Earth rotates on its imaginary axis while at the same time it revolves around the Sun, 3) The brain has billions of neurons and synapses, 4) Conception is the point when the nucleus

of a sperm cell joins with the nucleus of the ovum. The above are fundamental concepts that a person who only speaks a tribal language will find it impossible to comprehend, and the repercussion is that that person starts feeling inferior to anyone who speaks English. Unless the government can endeavor to develop tribal languages so that such statements are spoken in all our tribal languages, it should be the duty of the government to teach every citizen English so that they are empowered to explore for themselves the widest range of human knowledge. Since knowledge is power, no wonder all our government leaders speak English. If we truly want to empower the layman, let him know how to read and write in the most powerful language presently.

(5)   Moreover, speaking English will help people understand their tribal languages even better. Since we don't have a tribal alphabet, and instead we write our tribal languages in the English alphabet, knowing the alphabetical source of "tribal writing" is empowering to the person who speaks a tribal language. Because I can

speak English, I am able to deconstruct and analyze my tribal language Lusoga in a way that I would not have been able to. For example, it enriches my Lusoga when I can explain to anyone speaking any other language that "In writing Lusoga, the gerund is formed by changing the prefix of the infinite verb, unlike other languages like English or Spanish where you change the suffix of the infinite verb"

(6)   All tribal languages should be preserved by a nationwide literary campaign headed by the Chwezi Librarian (*see Chapter IV*). Indigenous languages can be official only at the local level because they can play a vital role in maintaining the local social fabric and economic development. However at the national and district level, English should be used with local language interpretation. Some politicians might want to make one of the tribal languages the national language, but this would be grossly unfair and a big disadvantage to the millions of Ugandans who are trying to acquire the most modern knowledge in today's world. To underscore this point, South Korea and

China, two countries that have well founded indigenous languages and indigenous alphabets, have aggressively embraced the knowledge (read power) potential of the English language. I have read that China wants to have at least 300 million people who speak English like native speakers by the year 2020, and in South Korea, some parents have their children's tongues elongated in surgical operations to make sure they can have flawless English pronunciation. Mind you those countries are not "losing" their indigenous language or forgetting their indigenous alphabets. In Uganda we have everything around us written in English, and all government officials speak English, but what a pity that most of the population cannot conduct international business because their English is un-intelligible. Or consider the fact that people in China or Japan or South Korea have to struggle to learn the English alphabet (because their languages are in non-Latin alphabets) in order to be able to program in computer languages, yet we in Uganda where the English alphabet is used in all our writing, we have not taken advantage of this fact to create a computer industry economic powerhouse.

Chapter III: The Fourth Republic

That means there is something fundamentally wrong. The main problem is that our leaders did not find time to define the issues confronting them. They borrowed foreign ideas and superimposed them on their countries: this could not, and did not, work. If you examine the scene in Africa, it is quite difficult to find a model solution. (Museveni, pg. 167)

Article 9. General Provisions.

(1)   Let the Chwezi Nation be a human heritage republic, unlike all the other countries of the world, which are mainly presidential republics or parliamentary republics. Presidential republics e.g. the US and most of the African countries are founded on three independent branches of government: the Executive, the Legislature and the Judiciary. This model of three branches was

created by the American politician James Madison – the father of the U.S Constitution—who created the general framework of the U.S government and national model. Parliamentary republics e.g. Japan, UK and most of the European countries don't have clear separation of power among the three branches because the Parliament forms the executive and also may act as the supreme court of law. And if you factor in the fact that most of such parliamentary republics have a monarch as the head of state, it is not clear how many branches those country's governments have. There are also semi-presidential systems like South Africa and France, which combine structures from both the presidential and parliamentary systems. Furthermore, there are countries like Saudi Arabia, which are absolute monarchies, whereby the King is also the Prime Minister and has absolute power. Lastly, there are theocracies like Iran whose national structures are based on a state religion where the head of the religion has absolute powers over all the decision of the state. Below are diagrams showing some of the governmental branches in today's modern world.

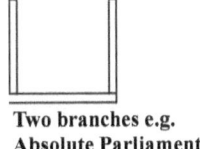
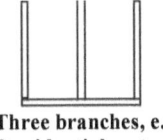
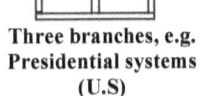
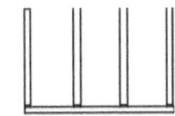

Two branches e.g.
Absolute Parliaments
+ and Monarchy

Three branches, e.g.
Presidential systems
(U.S)

Four branches e.g. 3
branches + a monarchy

Figure 1: Examples of Branches of Government

(2)   I am proposing a human heritage republic, which is divided into four branches of authority and two administrative divisions—see diagrammatic representation below. National authority should be based on the four separations: separation of Governance, Representation, Justice and Human Heritage. The four branches are demarcated into two non-political branches (the Human Heritage Branch and the Judiciary Branch), and two political branches (the Legislature and the Executive). The non-political branches are the most important branches of the republic because they play an impartial national role without getting involved in politics. The Human Heritage branch is a customary branch to highlight and incentivize the citizenry about the most important human pursuits that have led to the ascent of the human race: discoveries

31

and creations based on knowledge. The Judiciary is for interpreting the law to render universal Justice to all people, especially the minority and marginalized groups. There should be an impartial assessment of the four branches of national authority by Inter-branch offices.

(3)   Unlike the present worldwide branches of government mentioned above, let the symbol for the four branches of our national authority be as shown below.

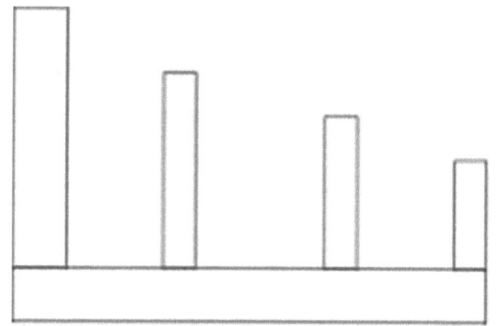

Figure 2: The Chwezi Branches of Government

Branch one represents the creativity in each individual; every person in the country should be given boundless opportunities to be creative and the state should not stifle people's mental processes. Branch two represents Universal Justice; every person in the country should be served justice at all times in all places. Branch three stands for people's political representation; every person's political opinions should be heard and voiced either verbally or through political associations. Branch four represents societal governance; once every person is free to be creative, is served universal justice and his/her political views are represented, the role of government will be minimized.

(4)   The following is my model of the Fourth Republic.

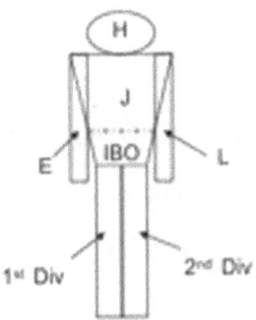

Figure 3: The Fourth Republic Model

H is for Human Heritage, J is for Judiciary, L is for Legislature, E is for Executive, IBO is for Inter- Branch

Offices, 1st Div is for Local Council administrative level, and 2nd Div is for District administrative level. Just as the head is the most important part of the body containing the brain (the organ that has made humans the most powerful species on earth because of our advanced neo-cortex), the Human Heritage branch which celebrates the humanity and creativity in our people will bring about the best that the Ugandan mind can come up with. Just as the chest contains the life-enabling organ (the heart), the Judiciary champions universal justice for each citizen because justice is what sustains a human life within society. Just as the human arms work together, the Executive and Legislature should balance each other by the former governing and the latter making sure there is accountability. And lastly, just as we stand on our legs and use them to get from here to there, the two tier administrative divisions are supposed to enable the citizens govern themselves and make direct socio-economic impact with no interference from government besides regulation. The Inter-Branch Offices help to give an independent and effective assessment of all power centers in the country.

ARTICLE 10. A CONSENSUS FOR OUR FOURTH REPUBLIC

(1)   In order to have a good nation, all that we need is a consensus on how our republic should be structured. History and the present world order illustrate that a people can form a great nation based on a wide range of different characteristic social values, the spectrum of which falls between social values based on collectivism on one hand and social values based on individualism on the other hand. Collectivism can come in the form of monarchism, class-stratification, family ties, tribes, or religions. In the political arena, collectivism is championed by doctrines based on socialism/communism or conservatism. On the other hand, individualism comes in the form of championing personal freedoms. In the political arena, individualism finds expression in doctrines that can be termed liberal or progressive. Between these two extreme ends of social valuation, i.e. collectivism and individualism, despite the fact that each camp professes to work towards achievement of equality for all members

of society, the debate is often centered on three motives: 1) to revert society towards a certain past glory, 2) to keep society as it is at the present time, and 3) to progress society towards a certain bright future. Though none of the three motives is utterly wrong and none is absolutely right, it is evident that political struggles are between agitators of either one of the two social values to achieve social equality by any of the three motives. In order to have a good successful society, there is no one attribute mentioned above that is superior or better. For example, western countries based on individualism have succeeded over many centuries but on the other hand Japan and other East Asian countries that are based on collectivism have succeeded in a short time. Nonetheless, the undisputed driving force for successful societies is that their people are hardworking, productive and creative citizens. In order for us to build a good successful society, we have to find stimuli to make our people hardworking, productive and creative. One such stimulus was covered in my book *The Fourth Heritage* in which I attempt to lay down a mental roadmap for the Ugandan individual. I believe that adherence to the thinking of the Fourth Heritage will bring about a consensus for our Fourth Republic.

(2)   On the National Day (*see Article 21 (2) for definition*), each region should pick to fly one flag color except the central region, which flies all three primary colors to signify our nationhood. The central region is the seat for the Heritage branch because that region is the historical center of Uganda and it should act as the symbolic unifying center irrespective of people's political views.

ARTICLE 11. OUR POLITICAL SYSTEM

(1)   Within our Fourth Republic, the political system should encourage individual merit besides multi-parties. This way, we shall have the stability and certainty that comes with strong personal leadership but also enjoy the benefits of pluralism and consensus building, which allow tolerance of varying opinions. The individual merit system will prevent stagnation in political parties and enable any

citizen who has the right idea at the right time to appear on the national scene and possibly fundamentally change the national system. A simple majority i.e. 50%+ should decide elections, while a super majority (66%) should decide constitutional/republic issues. All elections at all levels in the country should be by secret ballot. All citizens, whether in Uganda or in foreign lands, should have the right to vote.

(2)   Political participation should be voluntary and based on pragmatic non-ideological basis. To aid this non-ideological political process, people should have the right to participate in politics either in political parties or as independent individuals. No political party can be formed with a tribal or religious ideology. Political parties should be formed with the sole aim of delivering tangible benefits to the citizenry, benefits like good education, food, health, safety—no ideology is required to achieve these ends. Before national elections, political parties have to show evidence to the Supreme Court that they are non-tribal and non-religious by way of a threshold percentage of

electoral support in each of the four regions (*see lection section below for details*). Since cabinet members won't be active members of political parties, this system means that in parliament, there is no government or opposition, just MPs who are the legislature that are concerned with checking and balancing the executive. MPs from both the winning and the losing parties work as a unit to check and balance the executive. Because of this, the structure of the parliamentary chamber should be changed from its current west-minster model to a semi-circular model.

(3)   All national authority branches should come up with incentives to dissuade or regulations to prevent sectarianism, nepotism and family dynasties in national politics.

(4)   Political parties should be defined by the constitution. For example, each political party could be led by a National Executive Committee with a chairperson. The committee can have at most two people from one tribe and also at most two people from the same Local Council.

Whoever is elected by a political party to be on its National Executive Committee cannot stand for elective offices. If such a person wants to stand for national elections, she/he has to resign the NEC position for at least one year before he/she stands for a national office. This practice will enable people to get into political party leadership to champion specific policies and visions as opposed to merely using the party as a vehicle for national offices.

(5)   The definition of a political party is an organization formed to achieve specific political goals without changing the national system in a fundamental way. All political parties should be national, no regional based parties. The definition of a movement in this book is an organization formed by citizens to fundamentally change the system of the country. For example, the National Resistance Movement declared to have changed the country in a fundamental way starting in 1986. If parliament does not willingly adopt this new political paradigm, a new movement can be set up with the sole purpose of

fundamentally changing the system of the country in a more profound way than the 1986 change.

(6)   The President is elected by Universal suffrage. There are two Presidential terms, each consisting of four years. Parliament should enact a law that provides for public funding of elections and the minimization of the use of private money in elections. The use of excess private money could be curbed by having laws that call for all candidates to campaign together for the whole duration of the campaign season and also prevent private citizens from contributing a big amount of money to candidates. Bribery of voters using products and produce should be a criminal offense.

(7)   Election day for all national offices is two months before the National Day (*see article 21, (2)*). Campaigns for national and district elections should be carried out in English with tribal interpretations. Presidential nominations should happen in two stages: 1) Six months before election day, all political parties have to demonstrate to the Supreme

Court that they have a national composition, by securing at least 10% of registered voters in each region. This will ensure that we have utmost 9 parties that truly have a national following. An independent candidate who wants to stand for presidential elections has to be supported by 5% of registered voters in each region. 2) Three months before Election Day, each political party nominates a flag bearer who is registered with the Electoral Commission. The Electoral Commission is entrusted with funding the presidential candidacy of the party that gets 10% in each region or an independent candidate that gets 5% in each region. Each presidential nominee should register his/her manifesto, which is in terms of a four-year plan with the Electoral Commission and upon the end of the Presidential term, the Electoral Commission should publish a score of how much the President fulfilled his/her manifesto. In case no candidate gets more than 50%, a runoff between the front two candidates is held---within 4 weeks. The President is sworn into office (*see appendix for oath*) on the National Day after the Chief Creator customarily invites the President-elect to become the head of government.

(8)   Power is entrusted with the government according to citizens' will of political association, which is to be exercised rationally and voluntarily. People by virtue of being born in the country or to Ugandan parents, have the right and duty of political association. They can do it individually or in a political party. Any citizen can initiate ideas for the country, and the national structure should facilitate this, e.g. by having a small threshold number of signatures a person can collect in his/her Local Council in order for Parliament to hear and debate that person's ideas.

ARTICLE 12. CITIZENSHIP

(1)   As citizens, we are a product of the three heritages (Indigenous, Judeo-Christian Islamic and European), and a person is free to associate with any one of the three heritages or none of them.

(2)   Citizens from an early age should live by wonder,

skepticism and curiosity as opposed to command and order. Indoctrination of any kind, be it patriotic or religious, is to be rejected, except in times of war when the National Assembly can make a decree for the purpose of drumming up national patriotism. Citizens have the duty to defend the constitution and uphold the relevant specific laws at all times. Before any citizen can vote for the first time, she/he is obliged to say the *Oath of Allegiance* (*see appendix*). The citizenry should be given the necessary tools and taught to understand their obligation to complete the work of creating our national paradigm. Foreigners who want to become citizens must say the *Oath of Allegiance*. The country should offer incentives to attract the best people from all over the world to want to become citizens.

(3)   The citizenry should be looked at in three different categories, children (below 21 years), adults (21 - 75) and the Elders (after 75). For official purposes, youth are people between the ages of 16 to 32 years. Citizens should have a right to renounce citizenship at any time and regain it at any other time. Citizens should be able

to accept employment, honors or rewards from foreign entities without Government interference. Any East-African living in Chwezia should be referred to as a 'half citizen'. Half citizens, even if they cannot vote, have the same privileges as Citizens unless where it strains the state capacity. Non- East Africans living in the country should be referred to as foreigners. Citizens above 16 should have the right to participate in civic duties by way of voting. Elders should have the right to find bliss at the dusk of life.

(4)   All programs of a public nature should be funded by the government: any private contribution has to be made through a local court of law, but in no way is private contribution a reason for favoritism towards the person or group of people making the contribution. The state treasury should fund state elections; the district treasuries should fund district elections, and local treasuries should fund local elections.

(5)   Any citizen with an idea about the national model

has the right to appropriate accessibility through the channels of the state system to air out her/his idea directly or indirectly through any means necessary. Government should guarantee to provide convenience to such a citizen in exercising this right.

(6)   If parliament promulgates this new republican model, the Uganda constitution should be amended and transformed into Chwezia General Law. The Parliament is entrusted with making specific laws, which should always quote the clause or article of the General Law that they fall under. The General Law must be written in plain general language, which is easily understood by a Primary School pupil, however, specific laws should be written in terms understood by the target audience for which the law is written. The Penal code drawn up by Parliament should have language similar to that used for specific laws.

ARTICLE 13. DEMOCRACY AND REPUBLICANISM

(1)   The concept of the Fourth Republic is based on

democracy and republicanism. Democracy as a system means that all people participate in the election of all of their political leaders based on pure competition of ideas. Republicanism means that the country is governed by the rule of law and a non-hereditary head of state. Let our democratic republic not be defined by mere frequent elections, but rather by the national institutions we put in place. Let the election of the President be about change in policy and not about "eating the national cake"

(2) **Dictatorship of the majority**: Since many times, democracy degenerates into a dictatorship by the majority, our system should mitigate this problem by allowing minorities special attention and opportunity to petition the Courts about issues they feel are unfair due to the probable disenfranchisement by the majority. Any issues or a conflict that is concerned with democracy or republicanism is a fundamental constitutional issue that should be handled by the Supreme Court.

(3) **Republic Vote**: This is a nationwide vote

comprising eight votes whereby the general population has four votes, and each of the four branches of state has one vote. In order for an issue to pass a Republic Vote, it has to have seven out of eight votes. For each of the five electing entities, the vote should have a 66% margin of approval in order for an issue to pass. Any measure to change the constitution or the setup of the Fourth Republic or the election of the Chief Creator should be subject to a Republic Vote.

(4)   Our country should uphold democracy and personal freedom as fundamental principles. Personal freedom is a natural right, and not a privilege granted by the state. As such, this right should be inalienably practiced by free inquiry, free expression, pragmatism and limitless curiosity.

(5)   Each citizen in our democracy should be allowed the opportunity to pursue her or his emotional, intellectual, spiritual and material personal pursuits to the individual's satisfaction without obstacle by the government, as long as

public well-being is not threatened. People need to be free in order to reach their greatest potential and democracy is the best system to check a leader's shortcomings. Hence, the country should strive to balance the merits of democracy and freedom with the requirements of building a strong republic.

(6)   We should abandon the history of using the military in any way during national elections. Soldiers should realize that their role is to protect and secure, without prejudice, all citizens participating in politics. It would defeat the spirit of the fourth republic if some citizens are prevented from free political participation due to military force.

ARTICLE 14. NATIONAL GOVERNANCE

(1)   The role of the state should be to protect the weak people from exploitation by the strong people, but give the strong people opportunities to advance society. The constitution should be written to guarantee rights to

all individuals especially minority groups. Therefore, the laws of the land will be based on rights instead of absolute governmental power.

(2)   The Government should always uphold humanity in its diverse, yet similar forms, above anything else and it should ensure that a society is formed where every person has equal opportunity to find her/his place in life. And as a result, we shall be able to entrust public power with people according to their natural gifts or talents. People need to have confidence and trust in their leaders in order for the leaders to carry out good organization. Leaders in the country should uphold the fact that their duty is not to manage people but rather to empower people: a strong leader may create a weak people, but strong people don't need a strong leader. We should remember that the strength of our society will be judged by the strength of the weakest people among us. The fabric running through the realm of public authority should be values, ideas and institutions; no ideology is needed. Public authority should be divided into national

government, district administration and local leadership; where they come into conflict, the national government is the arbiter. With a firm reliance on the power of good governance, people aspiring for public office should have the option to join political organizations or stand based on personal merit. These aspirants should be offered equal state support. Any person should have the right to stand for any leadership position in the nation. Let the leaders be people elected because of their epistemic qualities as opposed to sectarian or identity politics.

(3)   National Assembly: There should be an annual 'Chwezia National Assembly' hosted in the Human Heritage building on the National day. It is attended by Parliament, the Cabinet, the Supreme Court and the Chief Creator (*See Chapter IV for details*). The National Assembly is a non-political summit to discuss national issues. The Chief Creator should chair the National Assembly. In time of emergencies, e.g. in a state of defense upon foreign invasion, the National Assembly is the highest seating of authority and by a vote of 3 out of 4 (each vote being held by a national branch), it can make National decrees that can override any law in the land.

(4) **State Assembly**: There also should be a semi-annual 'Chwezia State Assembly' when Parliament is joined by the Cabinet and District Administrators. The State Assembly is a political summit chaired by the President of the cabinet.

(5) The National Government should come up with a list of national public holidays. One of the holidays should honor 'Unknown Heroes': people who did great things and created our cultural norms and customs thousands of years before the modern era of written history. The government should decide which international public holidays to observe.

(6) Our nation should uphold the separation of faith and state. The government should be secular and will not participate or interfere in people's religious activities. However, government officials can officially participate in

cultural or traditional activities. Individuals can organize religiously according to their interests and means and government should make sure they have religious rights, except where the courts determine that specific religious activities are against the welfare of citizens, e.g. the mass religious suicide/murder at Kanungu in 2000 which killed over 1000 people.

(7)   The Country should pledge to abide by all laws of the international community at all times, except when Parliament decides that so doing would be a disservice to humanity.

ARTICLE 15. GOVERNMENT GUARANTEES

(1)   The government should guarantee to honor each citizen's *Oath of Allegiance* and all the rights and duties that come with it. Government should guarantee to educate the citizen to know that he/she is the nucleus and sovereign of the state. In light of this, government should never refrain anyone from forming opinions or

expressing them. Government should guarantee never to force or coerce the attainment of information from a citizen. Government should guarantee to respect the creative spirit in each one of us so that each person is educated and availed knowledge, which she/he can use to propagate the creation process in our republican paradigm. The government should guarantee that each citizen can obtain a passport in a very short time duration, preferably within days or weeks.

(2)   Government should guarantee to provide declassified information to any citizen who asks for it. Government should guarantee never to interfere in anyway in people's private lives or communication. Government should guarantee never to be part of or form a system/ bureaucracy so big and complex that an ordinary citizen cannot have immediate access through it. Government should enact specific laws and guide people in such a way as to elevate people from misconceptions brought about by any closed mindset system that is a historical cause of conflicts. Government should guarantee to serve the

citizenry in the best way that will nurture the growth of individual personality and uniqueness within a sociable community. The government should guarantee never to promote a personality cult or idolization of any human being in any way, shape or form: even the Chief Creator and the President should be looked at as fallible individuals with virtues and vices and not necessarily worthy looking up to in any way other than their constitutional duties. Hence, any person can be prosecuted for an offense at any time.

(3)   Government should guarantee justice that is free of charge and whose accessibility is universal. This justice could be legal, financial, emotional, or otherwise to satisfy the affected individual. Government should guarantee to avail equal opportunities to every citizen without negative discrimination in regard to gender, tribal, and other differentiating traits. Government should guarantee to prohibit any form of monopoly that would concentrate a lot of power in a few hands. Government should guarantee the same privileges to half-citizens as to citizens except

where it strains the state capacity. Government should guarantee to take care of children, the elderly and the most disadvantaged in society and give exclusive rights to women in matters pertaining to childbirth. Government should guarantee to emancipate women who undergo abuse and exploitation in the marriage institution. Government should guarantee all universal freedoms (e.g. movement, expression of opinion, assembly, worship) without partiality.

(4)   Public gathering should not require permission but only notification so that government can provide security and order.

(5)   People who don't wish to participate in the political process have a right as long as they don't threaten the common good and they pay for the government services they receive. People are free to be private citizens and not participate in public affairs.

(6)   Since freedom of thought is propagated by dissent

towards the prevailing status quo, government should guarantee freedom of dissent in all forms except where it calls for anarchy at which point only the courts are empowered to decide on an individual's right to dissent.

ARTICLE 16. COUNTRY DECLARATIONS

(1)   Outsiders called the country 'Uganda' because of the Buganda kingdom. In 1890, the country was declared a property of Imperial British East Africa Company, but four years later due to business circumstances it was taken over by the British Crown and declared a British Protectorate.

(2)   In 1962, the first republic was formed when we declared independence under a federal parliamentary system, but four years later the second republic was born when Obote declared the country a presidential republic. On January 29th 1986, the NRM declared a fundamental change of the Uganda republic and in 1995 the new constitution of Uganda ushered in the third republic.

In order to reach the next level, there should be a declaration to end the NRM's fundamental change so that we can usher in the fourth republic, a Human Heritage Republic.

ARTICLE 17. RENUNCIATION OF WAR

Due to our war-troubled history, the country should aspire for everlasting peace by renouncing the practice of war. Consequently, the country will be neutral. However, the Department of Defense will empower the defense forces in all possible ways to ensure defense of the citizens upon foreign invasion. Internal security is to be provided by the National Police. The super majority of the military should be in the reserve forces, but the defense department should meticulously plan for all reserve forces to be activated into a formidable standing military at short notice, upon foreign invasion. To help keep the military's morale high, the defense department should organize frequent competitive sports for all its members.

ARTICLE **18.** PROTECTION OF THE NATION

All Citizens should use any necessary means to protect our motherland. Government should look at protection of our motherland as equal to protecting humanity. The government should cherish human equality in three major ways: 1) Ensure that the citizenry understands and upholds the new republic paradigm from which rests the foundation of societal order. 2) Ensure that Chwezi cultures and traditions are respected in their diversity because without cultures we cannot achieve total liberty. 3) Ensure that every citizen has access to affordable education and healthcare, so that each citizen is healthy and has an inquisitive mind.

ARTICLE **19.** OUR BUSINESS COMMUNITY

(1)   Private individuals should lead our business activities. National policy and laws should regulate business activities only in order to safeguard the public from exploitation, to prevent monopolies and to protect the environment.

(2)   Since our business community is not competitive enough on the global stage, government should promote and protect it for the economic empowerment of the nation. But once local businesses get competitive, economic space should then be opened to the rest of the world.

ARTICLE 20. OUR HISTORY

(1)   As a people, we have historically known our past through oral tradition. Accordingly, we don't have one single national history but rather distinct histories of particular tribes. Science has revealed that we migrated to present day Uganda from other parts of Africa. We have evidence that the present tribes displaced the indigenous peoples of the country, the Pygmies.

(2)   It was much later after our migrations that Arabs, Europeans, and Asians came to have contact with us in the present area of Uganda. We all are Ugandans, but our beginnings are somewhere else. Unfortunately, our

oral tradition does not pin point out where exactly we migrated from. The only credible history of our cradle has come about because of the scientific disciplines like Archeology. Science has shed light and given us the opportunity to realize the commonality that we all share even if we are different tribes. Actually, if you go back as far as science has revealed, we know that the first human being evolved in East Africa (where our country is situated) about 200,000 to 400,000 years and spread out to other continents of the world over thousands of years.

ARTICLE 21. TIME AND CIVILIZATION

(1)   In our oral and written history, we are faced with two differing concepts of time, cyclic and linear. From the oral history, we have cyclic concepts of time whereby several important dates or occurrences are embedded in oral stories about events, things and people. For example, every tribe has customary stories based on seasonal timelines. There are other tribal peoples like the Native Americans who had very sophisticated cyclic

calendars that spanned thousands of years and demarcated numbers of days in a month and number of months in a year different from our present demarcations. The linear concept of time was introduced to Uganda by outsiders (primarily the Europeans) and it is characterized by references to absolute times e.g. this year is 2011 years since the birth of the Jewish man called Yeshua or Jesus, whom Christians call The Messiah or Christ. There are also other linear times that are not universal in our society, e.g. the Islamic calendar has this year as the year 1432, the Jewish calendar has this year as the year 5771. There are also Hindu calendars, which have this year not as 2011 but rather as 5000+. On the Christian calendar that we use, the first Anglican missionaries arrived in Uganda in 1879; Uganda was proclaimed a protectorate of the British Empire in 1895. As modernity takes root across all aspects of our society, we are abandoning the traditional cyclic nature of time in favor of the Christian linear calendar. However, it is important to note that if we were to go absolutely with the correct linear calendar, according to modern scientific findings, the earth has been around for 4.5 billion years and the universe 13.7 billion years.

(2)   Out of both the traditional cyclic concept of time with its unknown dates of events, and the linear nature of time keeping with its known dates of events, we should find one paramount date/event on which to center a national calendar - the beginning of our year. For example we could choose a paramount date to signify the day our forbearers migrated and settled in the various places of present day Uganda. We can call this day our National Day. We can decide to make the observance during the day stand for atonement whereby we remember the unfortunate results of displacement and conflicts between we the migrating tribes and the indigenous peoples of the Uganda, while the night observance can be kicked off by family dinners before the night-long celebrations of our collective humanity as various tribes and peoples of a new nation. From this initial national calendar date, the country can proceed to demarcate a national calendar for events like school terms, elections, public holidays,

etc. Even the current year 2011 we could officially start writing it as x2011, where x stands for the unknown time since the Chwezi dynasty or the time since the big bang. For a specific calendar date for the National Day we could think of using the most popular holidays, e.g. January 1 or December 25. Even if the equator passes Uganda and the equinox days (March 21/22 and September 22/23) should be the most important days, we arbitrarily use the northern hemisphere time demarcations because of the massive European influence. December 25 is 3 days after the European winter solstice (December 21/22, the shortest day in the northern hemisphere), and it is very significant in the Northern hemisphere because that is the day the sun starts shining longer, the days start getting longer. Pagan people in Europe used to celebrate the coming back of the Sun on December 25, which is 4/3 days after the shortest day in winter.

(3)   People should understand that there are non-religious scientific facts about time, which recommend more universal monthly demarcation like the proposed

International Fixed Calendar of 13 months with 28 days or the world calendar with a perennial time demarcation of 12 months with equal quarters. Also, people should know that there are several cultures that had weeks with different days. Even if the earliest record we have of a culture having a week with 7 days is Babylonia even before the captivity of the Hebrew people, ancient China had weeks with 10 days, the Igbo had weeks of 4 days, and the Egyptians had weeks with 10 days making a month 3 weeks long. The point of all this is to remind Ugandans that each group of people always demarcates time according to their customs and creations, everything about how we humans demarcate time is created by people. For example, some Roman leader subjectively decided that he did not like the then prevailing calendar where the year started with March and ended with February and instead he made the year start with January and end with December. In the old system, the tenth month had the prefix dec (which means tenth) hence December, the ninth month had the prefix nov (which means ninth) hence November, likewise Oct (eighth) was called October, Sept (seventh) was called September. These realities notwithstanding, we are used to thinking that December is the twelfth month, November the eleventh month etc, just because one person with power decided to arrange time the way he saw fit. Since the country sits right on the equator – the center of the planet, our earth scientists should study and revaluate the daily hour counting and accurately demarcate hours of the day and our national calendar.

(4)   Civilization is the creation of a complex structure of culture that is stable and powerful. Since Homo sapiens arose in Africa between 200,000 and 500,000 years ago, we lived nomadic lifestyles for most of pre-historic time. It is only 7,000-10,000 years ago that the first human civilizations were built, first in Africa, the Middle East and the Mediterranean coast, and then in China, India and the Americas. The most recent human civilization started in Western Europe about 1000 years ago, it had its golden days about 500 years ago under the Italian renaissance and the guiding arm of the Catholic Church and it has recently peaked with modern science, which has

produced the first-ever human explorations of the moon and other planets. Western European civilization has been the first human civilization that has impacted all the peoples of the planet, from Africa to the Americas, from Japan and Asia to all the Islands of the Oceans. Examples to show the extent of the Western European civilization impact can be seen in such facts as: the world follows a time calendar created in Europe, most of the land and waters of the world were named by Europeans, European political and economical systems dominate every corner of the world, and the modern scientific formulas and discoveries—formulas and discoveries that are the engine of the modern world— are greatly Western European in origin. Nonetheless, I think this civilization is under a lot of strain presently because even if its engine, modern science, continues to invent material products that make our lives better, there is not a center holding civilization together. Every civilization has a center, e.g. ancient Egypt had the Pharaohs and The Way, classic China had Confucianism, the Roman republic had the Senate, and the golden era of the renaissance had the Catholic Church.

Nowadays, it seems like our world civilization is centered on material consumption and narcissism, which are not the best center that can hold a people together, no wonder the personal alienation felt by the modern man.

(5)   I hope the creative proposals of the institutions in *The Fourth Republic* together with the ideas in *The Fourth Heritage*, can act as a center for building a durable civilization in Uganda.

(6)   Several systems have different arrows of time. For example the universe has the cosmological arrow of time which is 14 billion years old with the big bang marking the point of beginning, where you measure the before and after time periods; the Christian arrow of time has the birth of Jesus as the point where you measure before and after time periods. The following should be the Arrow of Time for our nation. From this arrow of time for our nation, we will re-orient our children's mind with a new narrative about our history in the big picture history of the world.

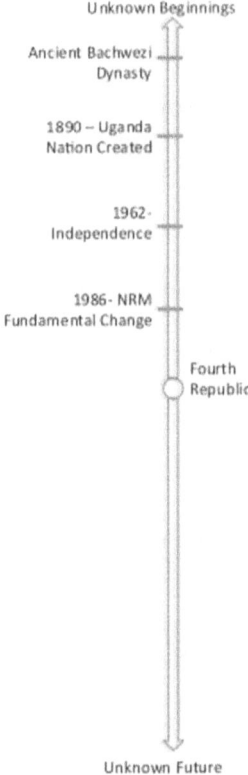

Figure 4: Uganda Arrow of Time

(7)   People should know that our country is located
on the African continent, along the equator, on planet
Earth; that the earth is just a very tiny object floating
in space around a star we call the Sun (the Sun is about
1,300,000 times bigger than the Earth); that there are over

400 billion stars in our galaxy and there are billions of galaxies in the known universe; that on Earth, the other four continents are Europe, Asia, America and Oceania OR when looked at as landmasses they are Eurasia, North America, South America and Oceania; that most of the earth is covered in water, the biggest water body being the pacific ocean which is bigger than all the continents combined; that according to the most advanced scientific consensus, the universe was formed about 14 billion years ago; that as humans we have not discovered or agreed on an absolute frame of reference for "time" and as a result "time" is relative even though many known civilizations measured time with their points of references being the Sun or Moon; that for simplicity reasons, people have come up with concepts like 60 seconds make a minute, 60 minutes make an hour, 24 hours make one day, 7 days make a week and about 4 weeks make up a month; that most calendars are either lunar or solar; that it takes about 365.25 days for our planet to go around the sun (hence the length of the earthly year), while it takes about 28 days for the moon to go around our planet; that every ethnic group

creates legends and myths about its own origin in which its people are a special group.

ARTICLE 22. OUR CULTURES

(1) In Uganda, we have four main tribal groupings: the Bantu, Sudanic tribes, Nilotic tribes and Kuliak (Atekerin) tribes. There are also non-tribal groups like the Asians.

According to the constitution of 1995 there are 56 identified tribes of Uganda, namely: Acholi, Alur, Baamba, Babukusu, Babwisi, Bafumbira, Baganda, Bagisu, Bagungu, Bagwe, Bagwere, Bahehe, Bahoroo, Bakeny, Bakiga, Bakonzo, Banyabindi, Banyankole, Banyara, Banyarwanda, Banyole, Banyoro, Baruli, Basamia, Basoga, Basongora, Batagwenda, Batoro, Batuku, Batwa, Chope, Dodoth, Ethur, Ik(Teuso), Iteso, Jie, Jonam, Jopadhola, Kakwa, Karimojong, Kebu(Okebu), Kuku, Kuman, Langi, Lendu, Lugbara, Madi, Mening, Mvuba, Napore, Nubi, Nyangia, Pokot, Sabiny,So(Tepeth), Vonoma.

(2)   According to the anthropologist Margaret Mead, there are three kinds of cultures: Traditional, Transitional and Learning Cultures (Woolman, 270). Traditional cultures are those that are closed, static, rooted in the past and controlled by elders. Transitional cultures arise and develop when traditional cultures are not adequate, they try to integrate knowledge from other systems. Learning Cultures are those in which voices of diversity and differences are welcome and respected: "agreements about the central ideas and values of the culture are formed by a pluralistic community and diversity is not a problem to be solved but to be appreciated for its own sake" (Woolman, 270). Uganda is one of the most diverse countries in the world in that we have over 56 tribes; our religions include Christianity (Catholics, Orthodox, Protestants, Seventh Day Adventists, Jehovah's Witnesses, Mormons, etc), Islam, Hinduism, Bahia, and Judaism. Let our cultures be Learning Cultures. Both of my books are a personal effort to transition our cultures from being oral traditional cultures to being book-based Learning

Cultures. We each belong to tribes, but we should never be tribal. I define tribal as being close-minded, being driven by ethno phobia, and favoring your tribesmen. We are born in tribal or religious molds, however unless we break free from those molds and impact personal interpretations of those traditions, we cannot totally realize our selves or our potentials. This is because when tradition becomes security, minds start decaying.

(3)   In line with the idea of "Learning Cultures", the country should officially recognize non-tribal citizens (e.g. Asians, Europeans) as rightful citizens with equal right as any of us because all our tribes at some point in history migrated from other areas of Africa to this land we call Uganda. There can also be people who might wish to abandon their indigenous cultures due to personal choice or children born of parents that don't belong to any of our traditional triples heritage. For example, a child born in Uganda to a Chinese father and an Indian mother is 100% Ugandan and a person who voluntarily abandons

all customs and associations with the tribe(s) of his/her parents is still 100% Ugandan.

(4)   Traditional leaders: Traditional leaders should not play any political role at all. Their duties are to uphold, but also more importantly, to transform our cultures. An individual should not be obliged to participate in any cultural traditions by leaders, unless he/she willingly chooses to do so. Traditional leaders should find audience on the national stage via the Human Heritage branch by way of nominating the Chwezi Librarian. Traditional leaders should not represent a geographical area, but rather a group of people, who could be anywhere in the world. In line with the provisions of Article 22 (2), traditional leaders have to remember that their cultures are not static—they are supposed to be Learning Cultures. Effort should be made by individual cultural leaders to culturally and intellectually progress their people without politicking.

(5)   During the national census, every citizen should

be given the choice of deciding to be identified tribally or not.

(6)   To clip the wings of tribalism and groupthink in our national affairs, one way we can get rid of identity politics is for all tribal affiliations and emotions to be channeled to the institution of the Chwezi Librarian via literary discourse (*see next chapter*). Per the guidelines of our Human Heritage republic, there should be no place for tribalism in political affairs. To put this in practice, our laws have to encourage, and the Judiciary should make judgments that build a national consciousness, so that people are looked at in respect to their ability rather than their ethnicity or birth. Since many of the evils of tribalism emanate from each tribe feeling special and seeing all other tribes as different if not inferior, by having tribal interests represented at the same platform, there will never be demonizing of other tribes by any tribe. Since our greatest weakness— what led to the imperialists colonizing us was the lack of a literary culture, the main role that tribal leaders should have is to transition our

75

tribes from oral cultures into literary culture via the Chwezi Librarian. Until that literary transition is finished, cultural leaders should have the humility to listen to us as we struggle to reconcile our oral heritages with the modern world of literary cultures. Each individual should embrace the fact that his/her cultural heritage is in his/her head and not necessarily in traditional leaders. This is my suggestion of how we shall evolve beyond tribalism. There should be a specific law, which opens traditional and religious leaders to be prosecuted in civil lawsuits for engaging in politics.

(7)   In line with the national value to eradicate tribalism, a non-indigenous citizen can seek justice from the courts for being discriminated against by indigenous cultural leaders because of cultural reasons. How I wish that the whole citizenry can be sensitized about such a national ideal akin to how the American public is sensitized about non-discrimination acts. In the U.S, it is common to find posted on business premises and other public places a poster that reads: "It is the policy and commitment of

THIS BUSINESS that it does not discriminate on the basis of race, color, sex, national origin, disability, religion, familial status, or source of income...." How I wish that in Uganda every business and citizen would be well versed with an ideal such as: "It is the policy and commitment of THIS BUSINESS that it does not discriminate on the basis of tribe, culture, regional origin or religion".

(8)   I thought about the idea of people seeking justice in the courts of law based on cultural discrimination because of the feeling I have towards the minority cultural groups within the country—people who will never have political power to make their interests heard by we the majority cultural groups. Of special concern to me are the super minority peoples (the Batwa and Bambuti) whom we call the pygmies, who were the initial inhabitants of this land we call Uganda. They occupy less than 0.05% of the national population because we the Bantu, Luo, Atekerin and Sudanic groups migrated to their cradle land and systematically we have occupied all livable areas of the

country such that the pigmies have had to escape into the mountains and deep forests to avoid ethno extinction.

ARTICLE 23. OUR RELIGIONS

(1)   Religions are traditions started by people to organize a systematic way of relating to God(s). Examples of these religions are Christianity started only about 2000 years ago, Islam started about 1400 years ago, Baha'ism started 160 years ago, etc. Tribal ways of relating to God usually are in the form of oral traditions. If those tribal traditions become written down, they are akin to Judaism (Hebrew tribes), Hinduism (Indian tribes) and Shintoism (Japanese tribes) where "the religion" is defined mainly by traditions as opposed to belief. All modern religions are based on books, and since the written word is more powerful than the oral tradition that all our tribes are based on, no wonder foreign religions have overpowered our traditional cultures and systems. Nonetheless, as outlined in Chapter II Pillar 2, all our tribes knew and understood God fully before foreign ideas of God where introduced

starting with Islam in the 1830s. Maybe in the next 160 years, or 1400 years or 2000 years some Ugandan person will come up with a systematic organized way of relating to God that could be called a religion. But until that time comes, respect and sensitivity should be rendered to the uneducated tribal masses as they struggle to reconcile their traditional tribal beliefs with the foreign religious beliefs that have harvested our souls. We, the young and educated generation, seem to have comfortably embraced the foreign teachings of Christianity and Islam, but lets have humility and ensure that we don't force our convictions on vulnerable people who don't read or understand the teachings of the Bible or Koran. The traditional non-religious people have a right to live life the way they choose even if most of their children go to Europeanized schools and adopt foreign religious convictions. These people are the carriers of our traditional heritages, which are thousands of years older than any religion; we must respect and honor them.

(2)   Since religion is a very personal private matter

concerned with certainty, belief and faith, while the fourth republic is an imperfect human arrangement by mere mortals, it is practically impossible for the citizenry to agree on one religious doctrine. Therefore, there should be no audience for religion in the affairs of the republic at any of the four branches of state or the two local administrative levels. The Fourth Republic is purely 100% secular. The republic is founded on a strict secular framework, but the state will ensure and protect every individual's religious practice. The laws of the country should protect freedom of worship without state interference.

(3)   Parliament or any other branch of the nation shall not have power to enact a law establishing a one party state or a religious state. And even if people have the right to believe whatever they want to believe, no one has the right to use their belief to engage in actions that harm or segregate against other people.

(4)   The only time religions can have a national presence is in some form of interreligious events coordinated not

by any political branch of government but by the Human Heritage Branch. Such events should be attended by all religions, including the minority religions within the country.

ARTICLE 24. REDEMPTION

(1)   In keeping with the traditional African concept of common humanity and Universal Justice, e.g. as expressed in the concept of 'obuntu bulamu', there should be a place within our justice system in which citizens that have committed atrocities against fellow citizens can petition the courts to be pardoned and redeemed into the general society. Before any trial, both parties should decide whether to go ahead with the prosecution or settle or seek redemption for the accused. The tribal concept of 'obuntu bulamu' is equivalent to what I was taught in Church that one of the greatest attribute of Jesus of Nazareth—the person that most Ugandans believe to be the Son of God—is the attribute of redemption for all human beings. I am sure other religious traditions

have equivalent figures that represent redemption. At a minimum, people who can benefit from our principle of 'obuntu bulamu' have to say the *Oath of Redemption (see schedules section)*. Such people have to work directly with their victims in a service capacity for a given length of time.

(2)   Also, in line with traditional African view of Justice, the criminal prosecution process should place more value on assistance for victims as opposed to the current justice system, which is heavily preoccupied with punishment for the offenders. Even if crime should be punishable, the goal is to look at human need and what the purpose of the law is, rather than simply putting a burden on people and condemning them when they don't live up to the law.

Article 25. The Individual

(1)   Each individual should realize his/her right to be innovative and creative in societal or personal matters,

and government should work on behalf of all citizens towards that end.

(2)   The concept of the Human Heritage Republic is to celebrate the supremacy of the individual who surrenders some of his/her supremacy to society, as represented by our institutions and laws, in order to promote the common good. The Constitution is entrusted with delineating and the Judiciary is entrusted with interpreting the balance between the supremacy of the individual and the requirements of the republic. The individual is the sovereign within the nation and as long as national institutions are set up with the individual in mind, we shall forever triumph over tribalism and groupthink. I believe that the framers of our national motto For God and My Country had this concept in mind when he wrote "My Country" as opposed to "Our Country": each individual should take ownership of our nationhood and contribute according to his/her personal talents. There cannot be any law that prohibits any individual from residing anywhere in the country or that disfavors any citizen from partaking

in matters of a civil or political nature in any part of the country.

(3)   Any individual should be able to rise through society to any position of leadership that they desire, without any systematic hindrance. How I wish all parents encourage their children from an early age – and all our children embrace as their highest goal— to grow up to become the Chief Creator of the country. That way, our children, wherever they might end up in this world, will keep working towards contributing to the creative enterprise that has been unfolding for the past 14 Billion years.

(4)   **Bill of Rights**: In order to safeguard the humanity of each individual, the government should accept the UN Universal Human Rights Declaration. Based on that declaration and also on our fourth republic ideals, we should draw up a Bill of Rights so that each citizen learns his/her natural rights, which are not a privilege bestowed by the state but rather self-evident innate rights arising

from nature. This Bill of Rights has to be translated into our tribal languages.

ARTICLE 26. OUR SOCIO-ECONOMIC SYSTEM

(1)   All the four branches of authority must work together and regulate to ensure that the market serves human values. This effort by our nation will help to check the evils that come with material consumerism. However, government should do this without stifling private enterprises because it is not the government but rather private companies that will contribute to our competitive edge in international business. The government should make laws to make sure there is minimum wage, no child or slave labor, devise a policy for unemployment insurance, ensure old people have pensions and workers have worker man's compensation. The government should work tirelessly to incentivize the citizenry to acquire a work ethic that propels the country to economic development, instead of patronizing people with handouts or tribal/ religious trivialities.

(2)   In the socio-economic affairs of our society, government should ensure that there is constant communication between national, district and local administration in all matters of public interests.

(3)   Citizens should be free and secure within our society. Every person should have an equal share of humanity and should be judged based on the nature of her or his ideas.

(4)   In matters of economic activities and business, government should compete with the private sector. Logically, government should have an advantage over private people because of the extensive nature of planning and resources available to government over many years. But since private people's strong natural self-interest will make them more efficient and more productive than the government, the government has to respect that reality. The same applies to labor; government should strive to have workers who are better off in comparison to private

sector workers, but since private citizens might have a stronger self-interest in acquiring the most advanced labor skills, the government needs to respect that.

(5)   Economic policy should be based on sound sustainable theories, monitored by the Sustainability Ministry. Government should provide affordable education, healthy care and public transportation to the citizenry. Government should come up with an effective and simplified money collecting system, where people pay taxes proportional to their means. Complicated taxation regimes should be discouraged. Taxation money should be divided three ways, whereby a third of the money goes to each of the three entities (Local Council, District, and National government). We should think about creating a new currency with an indigenous name because: a) many of our citizens due to tribal linguistic limitations, cannot pronounced the English word "Shilling", and b) the word Shilling is of a diminutive origin.

(6)   Government should be functioning 24 hours a

day, all days of the week, but an individual working for government should work for a limited number of hours per day e.g. 8 hours with appropriate breaks. Economic activities by both government and private people should factor in the difference between night and day so that specific activities are performed at the most optimal time. Government should not restrain workers and public servants from forming unions.

(7)   Is it possible to regulate the market to incentivize creativity by scaling monetary rewards for personal endeavors, e.g. in descending order we can scale remunerations so that activities showing creativity are rewarded most, then second are those activities that show discoveries, and lastly activities to do with vocations or entertainment.

Chapter IV: Non-Political Branches

The biggest problem we have had in Africa, however, has been lack of ideological independence. We are always running around following other people's definitions. (Museveni, pg. 244)

Article 27. General Provisions.

There should be two non-political branches of our republic: the Human Heritage Branch and the Judiciary Branch. The role of the Human Heritage Branch is to twofold: to preserve our cultural heritages and also indulge in intellectual creations that advance humanity irrespective of political leanings. The Judiciary is to deal with the Law and interpreting the constitution. In no way are these non-political branches to indulge in politics, except in time of war.

Sub Chapter One: Branch One - The Human Heritage Branch

ARTICLE 28. GENERAL PROVISIONS.

(1)   This is the branch with the highest civil authority—not power—in the Nation. However, all its decisions are mere recommendations, which could be accepted by Parliament with a 66% approval margin. This branch works with all non-political civil entities to preserve culture, harness human knowledge and empower the citizenry through education. Since knowledge is power, this branch will set our destiny as a nation. The first step in empowering the citizenry is to harmoniously preserve our trip heritages while at the same time creating opportunities that guide every single citizen in the perfection of their individual fourth heritage such that over time we shall

grow an original heri as outlined in my first book *The Fourth Heritage.*

(2)   The Human Heritage branch comprises three entities: The Head of State, The Chwezi Creators' Quorum and The Academy of Human Knowledge (*see the following articles for explanations of each entity*). The three entities can hold meetings in the Human Heritage Building (*see diagram below*). Official proceedings of the Heritage Branch can be carried out in any of our tribal languages with English interpretation for those that may not understand the respective tribal language.

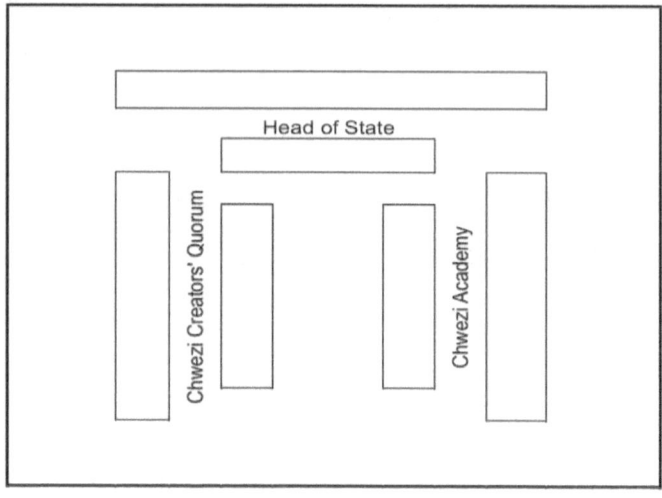

Figure 5: Human Heritage Building

ARTICLE 29. THE HEAD OF STATE

(1)   Let the head of the Human Heritage branch of our republic be the Head of State and the leader of our Nation. We can come up with a title for this position, but for this book, I will use the title "Chief Creator, Chancellor of the Universities and Leader of the Chwezi Nation". In short, I will call him/her The Chief Creator. He/she is the customary head-of-state of the country and Chancellor of all Universities in the Country. The head-of -state of our nation will be the person who, through his/her creative

powers, has created something that will advance our peoples in all our social and cultural differences. This is a very radical difference from the set-up of the present head-of-state position, which can only be occupied by someone who has financial and/or political power. The Chief Creator's office and home should be the State House, and it should be situated in the central region. Before assuming office, the Chief Creator has to say the *Oath of Chief Creator/Deputy Chief Creator* (*See schedules section*).

(2) **Election**: Private citizens have to be nominated by their Local Council - each Local Council has one nominee in elections organized by the electoral commission. Then from all initial nominees, each of the four national branches selects three finalists. The Electoral Commission organizes the final election on the National Day. Since it is possible to have duplicate final nominees, the number of nominees could be less than 12. By way of elimination, the National Assembly elects the Chief Creator and Deputy Chief Creators in a Republic Vote. Since the public will have initially selected all nominees, each nominee will be deemed to have the four votes from the general public. The successful candidates have to win at least three out of the four remaining votes held by Parliament, Cabinet, Supreme Court and the outgoing Chief Creator. In an election where the Chief Creator position is vacant, e.g. where the deputy Chief Creator is acting as the Chief Creator, the person who gets the most absolute votes among the three remaining national branches will become the new Chief Creator.

(3) **Tenure**: The Chief Creator's tenure should be a non-renewable term of five years.

(4) **Qualification**: The only qualification for the Chief Creator position is to demonstrate that you have created something. The person worthy being the Chief Creator has to demonstrate that he/she transcends tribal, political and religious ideology, and will not be biased towards a specific tribe, religion or political ideology. Since the overwhelming majority of Ugandans belong to a tribe or religion, aspirants should be judged on their tolerance or humanness in regard to these two criteria. Also, a potential candidate should be judged on his/her inclusive progressive politics that fight for the rights of minorities and the least among us. As people are most creative during their youthful years, there is no minimum age requirement, neither is there a maximum age limit. In case of a very young Chief Creator, the Deputy Chief Creators will carry out the national duties. It is imperative that we engender in our young people the aspirations to become Chief Creator of the country as young as their ages. This is because currently 56% of the whole population is under the age of 21 and what better positive stimuli for these young people than inspiring them to be creative in whatever endeavor they do, in the hope of being recognized nationally.

(5)   I define creativity as original mental processing that uses insight about existing ideas or concepts to produce something that adds value to the world. From reading about people that have been creative in many human endeavors, I realize that most of them fit a certain

age category. In the most universal human knowledge field of mathematics and science if you look at the ages of the major creative minds like Isaac Newton, Albert Einstein, Werner Heisenberg, John Nash, Niels Bohr, etc, you realize that creativity is highest before the age of 30. This rule also applies to modern creators in the modern computer industry where you find that Bill Gates (Windows' creator), Michael Dell (Dell Computer creator), Larry Page & Sergey Brin (Google creators) and Mark Zuckerberg (Facebook Creator) invented their products when they were in their late teens or early 20s. In the political arena, some of the events that have shaped and influenced the working of the world as initiated in America, were started by youthful individuals: George Washington led the war for American independence in his late 20s and become Commander in Chief at 33, Thomas Jefferson "the father of American democracy" wrote the Declaration of American Independence when he was 33, Martin Luther King Jr. took leadership of the American Civil Rights crusade when he was 26 years old. The following graph is my personal non-scientific representation of human creativity that has changed the world. By creativity I am referring to the mental processing of ideas and phenomenon. As evidenced in the Bronowski quote that follows the graph, I believe this creative mental processing starts in childhood, but since society purposefully discriminates against child thinking, creative people have to amass power in society somehow when they are much older in order for society to erroneously attribute their accomplishment to their adult positions.

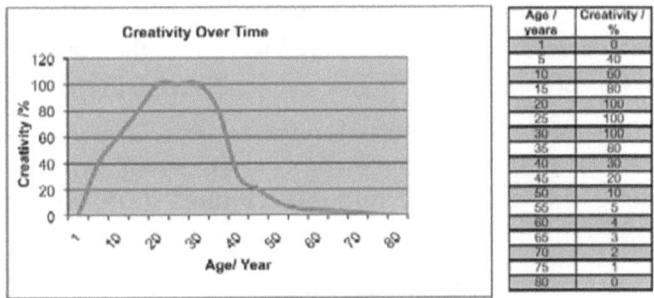

Age / years	Creativity / %
1	0
5	40
10	60
15	80
20	100
25	100
30	100
35	60
40	30
45	20
50	10
55	5
60	4
65	3
70	2
75	1
80	0

Figure 6: Creativity Versus Age

(6)   To underscore the importance of the young mind for the progress of humanity, I want you to intimately

digest the following words of wisdom from the eminent

Mathematician and scientist Jacob Bronowski.

The brain and the baby is where it begins. The ability to plan actions for which the reward is a long way off is the central thing that human brains have which there is no match in animal brains…That means that we are concerned in our early education actually with the postponement of decision. We have to put off the decision making process in order to accumulate enough knowledge as a preparation for the future… Biologically a human being is changeable, sensitive, mutable, fitted to many environments and not static. The real vision of the human being is the child wonder… For most of history, children have been forced to conform to the image of the adult. The ascent of man has never come to a stop, but the ascent of the young, the ascent of the talented, the ascent of the imaginative were halted many times. …Who am I to belittle the civilization of Egypt, of China, of India, even of Europe in the middle ages? And yet by one test they all failed, they limited the freedom of the imagination of the young. They were static, and they were minority cultures. (*The Ascent of Man: The long Childhood*)

We need to prevent our country being functionally static by creating a national model, unlike any other country, which relies on the natural creative power of the young people. According to Bronowski, only a fraction of the human intellectual talent that is found in a child's imagination is actually used. Society systematically discriminates against childhood, and forces children to conform to lowly adult traits. People grow up slowly climbing the ladders of social authority and when they reach the top, they become static without innovative ideas to change the status quo, because the only voice they start hearing from God is "now that you have reached the top, the last commandment is thou shall not question [or change]!" The main idea that describes the vision I have for the country is that we have, as the head of state, a person who embodies the greatest achievement of the human brain: creativity. The present national model has the head of state as someone who has amassed power either financially or politically, not someone who has excelled in creativity. Whereas raw power creates personal wealth and prestige, creativity creates enduring culture and civilization.

(7)   The following diagram is my personal artistic rendition of creativity within societies.

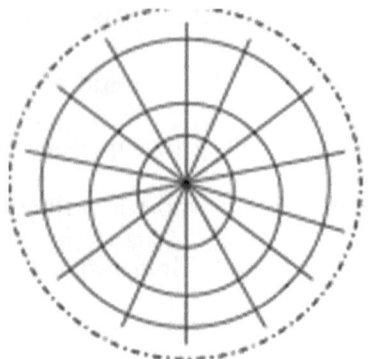

Figure 7: Creativity Model

Society is usually conservative and closed minded, like the circles. But within societies, there are individuals, represented by the lines, who aspire for greater and newer ideas. It is such individuals who enrich and develop society and enlarge the circle. Unfortunately, all changes in human history, changes we take for granted nowadays, did face a lot of resistance. For example: in politics, the American and French revolutions were resisted, but now the republics they produced are, to a great extent, the beacon of secular citizenship that defines modern democracies. In religion, the founders of the two major religions in Uganda (Jesus for Christianity and Mohammed for Islam) were initially rejected, but presently, more than 95% of the country is either Islamic or Christian. In science and engineering, Einstein's theories of relativity were rejected by the general public, and he was faced with death threats during his lifetime, yet now all humanity (Jews, Christians, Muslims and other peoples) enjoy the fruits of his genius. Also, before 1947, most Engineers and Scientists resisted the idea that planes could travel at the speed of sound, but now we take for granted the fact that supersonic modern air force jets routinely break the sound barrier.

(8)   Because creations are so important, it is no coincident that the most economically developed countries are the leaders in product and process creations according to Intellectual Property claims. The World Intellectual Property Organization's annual report shows that the two overwhelmingly greatest leaders in patent filings every year are Japan and the U.S.A; these countries are also the strongest economies of the world, and whichever country can overtake them will do it based on more creations- the way China is closing the gap.

(9) **National Duties:** The Chief Creator coordinates all human creations and discoveries by Ugandan citizens both within the country and outside the country. These creations and discoveries can be in any activity of human endeavor, i.e. academics, business, art, music, etc. The Chief Creator (just like any other citizen) may propose updates to the institutions of the Fourth Republic or may propose a Fifth Republic which measure has to pass a Republic Vote (*See section on Republic Vote in previous chapter*). Let our Fourth Republic constitution be a non-terminal constitution. While there are organizations that claim to be the final/terminal arrangement of human affairs, our republic should be dynamic in nature by encouraging that in the future someone might create a more perfect Fourth Republic or create the Fifth Republic. This way, all our children will grow up yearning to improve on the general setup of our society. Similar to the United Nations Resolutions, the Chief Creator, the Creators' Quorum and the Academy can make Human Heritage Resolutions that they submit to Parliament for promulgation. At a minimum, the Chief Creator should write a paper or book about a personal interest during his/her tenure. But to prevent national propaganda, the subtitle of the work should always read " A Personal View" so that citizens realize that they also have their own views about the subject, which might be different from the Chief Creator's views. The Chief Creator should frequently engage in educative activities with children. If Parliament declares a state of national defense, the Chief Creator becomes the Commander-in-Chief of all defense forces, but during peace time (*the country will be neutral, see previous chapter*), the Defense Permanent Secretary is the Commander-in-Chief of the defense forces. After a presidential election, the Chief Creator, upon advice of the Supreme Court invites the person who can head the government. The Chief Creator should be the coordinator of all charity and philanthropic activities in the country. Rich people should be incentivized to donate to charity instead of them amassing wealth for family members because often times, too much wealth inherited from parents can corrupt children's virtues. In this regard, we should consider having a very high percentage estate tax so that upon death, a big portion of a rich person's wealth is taxed. Every year the Chief Creator, upon recommendation by the Supreme Court, will honor individual Ugandans who have distinguished themselves in personal achievement or creativity. The accomplishments cannot be in politics and former politicians cannot get recognition for something they did while in politics. These Ugandans are to become members of the Chwezi Creators' Quorum. The cabinet on recommendation of Parliament honors political achievements with our national awards already in place.

(10)   National Corp of Engineers: The Chief Creator should coordinate the various Engineering professions in the country into a Corp that designs and builds Infrastructure in the country. The Corp will have to fairly compete with private firms in all Infrastructure projects.

(11)   National Corp of Doctors: The Chief Creator should coordinate the various Physician professions in the country into a Corp that should device means and ways to eradicate the country of all preventable diseases. The

Corp will have to fairly compete with private firms in the delivery of these services.

(12)   The Deputy Chief Creators: The two Deputy Chief Creators deputize the Chief Creator in all functions. Upon vacancy of the Chief Creator position, each deputy Chief Creator becomes Chief Creator for half the remaining term, and that time does not count as first term.

ARTICLE 30.THE CHWEZI CREATORS' QUORUM

This is the dynamic leg of the Heritage Branch. It will be the national forum for creativity and the evolution of our diverse human heritages. The Chwezi Creators are individuals who have excelled in creating ideas, processes, works or things that benefit all our citizens irrespective of tribe, religion or colonial heritages. I propose that the first two Chwezi Creators should be Philly Bongoley Lutaaya for his creativity in music and his heroic life witness in the fight against AIDS, and George Wilberforce Kakoma for his creation of the National anthem which in 1962 prophetically looked at our future which we must fulfill now with a more perfect nationhood. Each Chwezi Creator is nominated by the Chief Creator, seconded by the Supreme Court and appointed for life by Parliament. The Creators have no national duties, other than being examples to all of us, in how to excel in human endeavors. Before taking up the position, each new member of the Quorum has to say the *Oath of Human Heritage* (*See schedules section*).

ARTICLE 31. CHWEZI ACADEMY OF HUMAN KNOWLEDGE

(1)   This is the other leg of the Human Heritage Branch. It is to be made up of citizens with expertise in a particular area of human knowledge. They can be residing inside or outside the country. The Academy has ten members called Commissioners who are nominated by the Chief Creator, seconded by the Supreme Court and confirmed by the Parliament. The Commissioners' tenure is five years, renewable indefinitely. The Commissioners

are divided into five functional members; four head the four knowledge areas described below and one heads the Sports & Recreation department, and five managing members. Over the years, members may rotate between being functional and managing members. The most important task for the academy is to draw up the syllabus for all levels of education in the country.

(2)   There are four knowledge areas under the academy, namely: a) Mathematics, b) Natural Sciences, c) Social Sciences, and d) Humanities and the Arts. These areas have been selected to aid in harnessing and increasing modern non-tribal human knowledge (indigenous tribal knowledge will be addressed by the Chwezi Librarian). An alternative categorization of human knowledge is the findings in Howard Gardner's book *Frames of Mind: The Theory of Multiple Intelligences*, which delineates knowledge into: Verbal-Linguistics intelligence, Music intelligence, Logic and Mathematics, Spatial Intelligence, Bodily-Kinesthetic intelligence, Naturalistic intelligence, and Personal Intelligences. Before each National Day, the academy votes for the best University student in each

of the four knowledge areas and the four students are recognized and given prizes by the Chief Creator during celebrations on the National Day. We should come up with other non-academic areas for which prizes will be given, for example, sports.

(3) **The Chwezi Librarian**: He/She is the head of the National Library. Cultural leaders nominate, and the Chief Creator appoints the Chwezi Librarian for the time duration of the Chief Creator's tenure. The Chwezi Librarian should keep the official written history of our collective cultural groups. The Chwezi Librarian should oversee the writing of our history starting with the scientific natural history then our oral history that begins with the Bachwezi dynasty and lastly modern written history. The office of the Chwezi Librarian will act as the main entity that facilitates the transition of our oral cultures into written cultures. The Chwezi Librarian office will act as the conduit between our oral traditional cultures and peoples on one hand and the modern literary world on the other hand. We can use these four stages to transition our cultures from oral to written. **State 1** (1 to 2 years after implementing this model): we should ensure that every citizen can write the alphabet A to Z, his/her name, the name of the town, and the name of the country. **Stage 2** (1 to 5 years): we should ensure that every person can write the names of all the tribes and religions of Uganda, the names of all the continents and oceans of the world and the names of all the planets in the solar system. **Stage 3** (1 to 10 years): we should ensure that all old people in the country, especially those that cannot read or write, are interviewed and their oral history archived at the National Library. Also, we should ensure that every person can read the Constitution and the lyrics to the National Anthem. **Stage 4** (1 to 30 years- one generation): we should ensure that every citizen can read a small book.

(4)   Also, each tribe and clan should write down everything during cultural/traditional ceremonies, so that those accounts are forwarded to the National Library for archival purposes. This way, we shall have tribes learn

from one another and also have Ugandans outside of the country be able to connect to their tribal heritages via accessing the National archives. For example in my tribe we have a great tradition whereby when someone dies, people of the village join the mourning by spending 40 nights camped out over a bond fire at the bereaved family's home. While they drink, entertain themselves and remember the dead person, they play a great part in comforting the grieving family. As a young teenage boy, this tradition played a great role in comforting me and my young sisters during the trying period of mourning our father, but I know such a tradition might not work in a modern city setting. I would love for other tribes and cultures to know of such traditions so that we can further study them and indeed improve on them. One such improvement could be to recommend that people who work far away in offices in cities could participate by sending money or personal notes to be read at the bonfire. Also, unlike in the present time in which many of our cultural practices are done at night and mostly in the dark, we should construct buildings of stone and brick so that all our cultural practices are done in the open either in the light of day or in well-lit settings at night. This new development will slowly lead to the evolution of our cultural traditions from primitive practices to knowledge- based modern practices similar to Japanese Shinto practices. The national government should ensure that there is free movement of people around the country so that the diversity in every town and village will lead, over-time, to the creation and incubation of a national Chwezi cultural identity and dispensation.

(5)   National Library and other Public Libraries: The Academy is entrusted with building the National Library and other Public Libraries throughout the country, and populating them with books from all human cultures. The best way to help the poor and marginalized people is not to give them charity but rather to ensure that there is a public library in each village and town, so that they can help themselves. The arrangement of books in the libraries should cover: a) Tribal knowledge, b) Religious knowledge, c) Academic subjects (Mathematics, Natural

Sciences, Social Sciences and Humanities & the Arts), and 4) Personal Knowledge. We should come up with an original Chwezi Library system for the arrangement of these four knowledge categories.

(6)   Planetariums: The academy also is entrusted with building and operating at least one Planetarium in each region, where children can go to look at and learn the vastness of our immediate universe so that from an early age they develop grand imaginations and wonder about 'our world'.

ARTICLE 32. EDUCATION SYSTEM

(1)   The education system in the country should strive to improve the minds of the people at any price. However, due to the fundamental pillars of the republic, education cannot be a tool to propagate any single doctrine whatsoever, neither tribal, religious nor political. The Academy implements and monitors the education syllabi at all levels of national education. Education or Knowledge

is the main tool that can enable people transcend their limiting biological instincts and the most important tool that will bring about a hardworking, productive citizenry. The academy should have the right to challenge any state organ about matters that it feels do not help improve the intellect of the citizenry. National education should be geared towards a society of independent free thinkers who possess the relevant tools to propagate the process of creation in their own lives and also for humanity. The academy should coordinate with the Chief Creator to build at least one public library in each Local Council.

(2)   From the very first stages of schooling, children should be taught and shown our immediate universe constituting of the solar system and planets to help with the development of their imagination. I humbly implore our leaders to ensure that before any indoctrination of children's minds, the children are taught the discoveries of the natural sciences so that from an early age the children nurture imagination, curiosity and awe at the physical universe to which our planet is a small part of. I

can imagine infinite possibilities for our children if from their earliest years of schooling they get the opportunity to learn about the 10,000 years of human civilization on all the continents of the planet, or the billions and billions of galaxies in the known Universe or the 14 billion years of evolution of the Universe that modern science has revealed. However, since mythology is very important in every culture, we should continue teaching our children the myths and legends of the first man and woman being Kintu and Nambi, the cause of death being Walumbe, the stories of Ruhanga or Katonda creating the world, and other imported myths like Santa Claus (Father Christmas).

(3)   Religious education should go beyond the teaching of the two majority religions: i.e. Christianity and Islam. It should cover other world religions like Hinduism, Buddhism, Shintoism, Bahia, Judaism etc. In fact, religious education should be called 'World Religions and Spirituality' so that spiritual but non-religious ways of knowing God might also be covered; here I am thinking

about the tribal and scientific concepts of God that might not be covered in the present religious education. We know religions can be good for people. The teaching of world religions will enable people to explore the different religions of the world and settle on a religion that satisfies their spiritual longings.

(4)   Sports, music, dance and drama should be incorporated in the education curriculum.

(5)   The academy should ensure that all students studying within the geographical country or citizens studying abroad get the necessary resources. The academy has the duty to ensure that there is equal opportunity for both poor and rich children to attain good education at all levels.

(6)   Education levels should largely remain as they are structured i.e. Pre-Primary, Primary, Secondary and University. But we should add a gap year between O level and A level or between A level and University where

our young people can pursue non-academic personal adventures that could greatly help in their maturing into independent universal individuals or transition them from close-minded tribal peoples into open-minded global citizens. Along this reasoning, we could look into changing A level e.g. whereby the first year becomes a gap year and then the second year is added to University so that students have a generalized education their first year of University. University scholarships should also cover non-academic activities e.g. sports. University education should be 100% universal such that our universities can draw students from all countries of the world to study world-class courses.

(7)   It is important that we create an education system that is not based on students memorizing facts to pass exams but rather let us create a system that gives students the freedom and space to explore their natural intelligence (which might not always be tested on exams) so that students enrich their intellectual faculties and create ideas or things that fit their personal natural inclinations. Education

should be about students' aptitudes so that there is enough time spent on non-academic pursuits like social activities, community service, sports and personal initiatives. Our education system should not produce students who lack the whole human experience due to their obsession with passing standard tests. Education should be principled on teaching students skills for analysis and creation/ innovation as opposed to memorizing facts. Socrates once said that "at birth, each soul knows everything there is to know in the Universe", in line with this adage, teachers should realize that instead of suffocating children's imaginations by forcing facts into their heads, the teacher's role is to give opportunities for children to develop their curiosities and imaginations—which are the sources of true knowledge. We should keep the aggregate grading scale of 1 to 9 so that there is a wide enough range to gage students. From primary to secondary school, each student should have equal exposure to science and the arts.

(8)   The education system should be set up such that people who might not get a formal education can also join

higher institutes of learning if they prove capable. It is possible that some parents can teach their children at home better than in school or that some genius children might actually be able to educate themselves by reading books or learning on the internet without the need of a formal institution. There are a lot of examples from history where people who contributed to human intellectual advancement never had formal education, a good example is Benjamin Franklin who had only two years of formal education but he made profound discoveries about electricity and went on to be one of the greatest writers and publishers of his time, and was also maybe the greatest founding father of the U.S.A.

(9)   The national education should be set up so that children can learn in classrooms or at home on the Internet. With an Internet based education, children are free to learn on their own at their own pace but with guidance from parents and teachers. Teachers can still go to classrooms to teach students who want to learn in schools. However, to ensure that both home schooled students and classroom

students are learning at the same pace, the school system will need to have frequent periodic tests—which should not be based on memorization. Home-schooled students will be required to show up at school for some mandatory classes like Physical Education and debates, to aid in their socialization.

(10)   Since the country does not have a four-season climate that has a beneficial factor due to the cyclic changing of the seasons between winter and summer, we should stimulate it by organizing our school and economic activities factoring in the climatic changes between our two seasons. The rainy seasons are March to May and October to November, while the dry seasons are June to September and December to February. The school calendar should take advantage of our dual climatic seasons by having school and holidays rotate between the rainy and dry seasons. Our school calendars should not be mindlessly tied to the calendars of countries in temperate climates, which have four seasons.

(11)   Pre-primary and primary pupils should be taught their Indigenous language and Culture on top of English. They should be taught the natural history of the universe and also the history of all humanity since 10,000 years ago. The national government should fund teaching of English, but Local Councils with coordination by the Chwezi Librarian should fund the teaching of indigenous languages and cultures.

(12)   O level students should be taught at least one of the other International languages e.g. Portuguese, German, French, Spanish, etc). Also, every O level student should be taught the "History of Science and the great Scientists" so that both Arts and Science students know about the sacrifices made by the great minds behind the excellent scientific creations whose fruits all human beings enjoy now. After O level, students should have the option of attending vocational institutes or colleges besides aiming to go to University. If we continue with the A level system, 'A' level curriculum should be extended so that Science

students are also taught some Humanities/Arts courses and Arts students are taught some Science courses.

(13)   Schools should stay divided into Government Schools, those that get money from the government, and Private Schools. Both types of schools should teach from the same curriculum. Private Universities and Schools should be independent institutions without government interference.

ARTICLE 33. DEPARTMENT OF DEFENSE

The Department is responsible for safeguarding the country upon foreign invasion. The duty of safeguarding the citizenry during peacetime is bestowed upon the National Police. The country should declare military neutrality towards all other countries. The Department is in charge of managing the Chwezi Defense Forces (Land forces, Water Forces and Air Force). Participating in any branch of the Defense Forces is a service, which the nation should incentivize all able people to partake in.

The Permanent Secretary for Defense is the Commander-in-Chief of the defense forces during peacetime. The Chief Creator becomes the Commander-in-Chief if the National Assembly declares a state of defense. The Chief Creator nominates the Permanent Secretary and the Chief of Defense Forces, who are then seconded by the Cabinet before being confirmed by Parliament for a term of five years. Citizens can own guns pursuit to an act of parliament. The military cannot take part in partisan politics and does not play any role during elections. The National Police offers security during elections. There should be a National Security Council chaired by the Chief Creator and comprising the following statutory members: The President and Vice Presidents, The Speaker of Parliament, the Permanent Secretary of Defense, Chief of Defense Forces, Internal Security Organization leader, External Security Organization leader, National Police leader, Internal Affairs Minister and other non-statutory leaders selected by the Chief Creator and the President.

ARTICLE 34. DEPARTMENT OF HEALTH

The Department is responsible for promotion of a healthy living and safeguarding the health of the population by investing in disease prevention and control. The Permanent Secretary is nominated by the Chief Creator, seconded by cabinet and confirmed by Parliament for a five-year tenure.

ARTICLE 35. OTHER NON-POLITICAL OFFICES

The following are other national offices or institutions that should be apolitical. Their leadership is nominated by the Chief Creator, seconded by the Cabinet and confirmed by Parliament for a term of five years.

- Governor Bank Of Chwezia
- Human Rights Commission
- The National Police Force
- The Prisons Department
- Criminal Investigation Department
- Internal Security Organization
- External Security Organization

• The Post Office

Sub Chapter Two: Branch Two - The Judicial Branch

ARTICLE 36. GENERAL PROVISIONS.

This is the second non-political branch, which is concerned with interpreting all the laws of the land. The Supreme Court heads the judiciary. All members of the judiciary have to say the *Oath of Judiciary* (*See schedules section*). All Judges and Justices of the Judiciary can be impeached and removed from office by Parliament (for national courts) or by the Judicial Service Commission (for local courts).

ARTICLE 37. THE SUPREME COURT

The Supreme Court should have 9 Justices who cannot be part of the Judicial Service Commission. For the sake of diverse opinions in law matters, Justices can be from any sector of the public—that is to say, Justices don't have to be lawyers or legal experts. Justices are nominated by the Chief Creator, seconded by the Cabinet, and confirmed by parliament for a term of 9 years, renewable once. All Supreme Court Justices are equal in stature, but the Chief Justice is the first among equals. The Chief Justice in a one-year rotating position.

ARTICLE 38. JUDICIAL SERVICE COMMISSION.

This is an independent body whose composition is nominated by the Chief Creator, seconded by the Cabinet and confirmed by parliament. The tenure of membership should be longer than two presidential terms, non-renewable. The commission makes recommendations to the Chief Creator about non-supreme court judicial issues e.g. judicial appointments below the Supreme Court, judicial administration etc.

ARTICLE 39. THE COURT SYSTEM

(1)   The Court system should remain a four tier system, but with minor changes. Upon advice of the Judicial Service Commission, the Chief Creator nominates, and

parliament confirms, all the Justices and Judges of all the Courts below the Supreme Court.

(2)   Let the Supreme Court be the highest court in the land for all laws including the constitution. It should have one seat either in the East, West or North region. The Supreme Court should be the final appellate court for the Court of Appeals. The only cases it has original jurisdiction are constitutional cases, elections of the Chief Creator and the President, and issues pertaining to the nature of the Fourth Republic.

(3)   Let the National Court of Appeals be the second highest court in the land whose sole jurisdiction is to act as the appellate court for High Court cases. Justices of this court do not sit on the Supreme Court. Their tenure should also be 9 years renewable once. The National Court of Appeals has a seat in each of the four regions of the country. A Principal Justice heads it.

(4)   Let the High Court be the third highest court in the

land, which adjudicates national issues. The High Court should remain as dispersed across the country according to population distribution. Its members should be called Judges of the High Court. Their tenure should also be 9 years renewable once. A Principal Judge heads it.

(5)   Let the lowest courts in the land be called Local Courts at each Local Council. Magistrates head these courts. The Judiciary Service Commission should bundle several Local Council courts to be overseen by a Chief Magistrate. The Chief Magistrate's court is the appellate court for the subordinate Local Council courts.

(6)   Other Court Systems: There should not be any other court systems in the country. Any traditional or religious based courts have to be indigenous in origin and have to prove that their view of justice is universal, i.e. applies equally to all peoples. This issue of other court systems must pass a Republic Vote.

(7)   Any citizen at any time can be prosecuted for a just cause as stipulated by the specific laws without prejudice or discrimination. Parliamentary acts made either to protect or punish, should take on equal treatment towards all citizens. A citizen should be looked at as innocent until proven guilty by a public court of law. All court hearings should be public. All laws in the country (criminal, civil, administrative and constitutional) should be laws made by man, i.e. legislated by parliament and interpreted by the Judiciary. Because of the separation of faith and state, any natural law or divine law will be respected, as it is a non-negotiable matter between an individual and his/her interpretation of Nature or God. The state cannot legislate on natural or divine law, and conversely, natural and divine law cannot be used to subvert state laws. Under state law, any citizen, irrespective of tribe or belief will be treated as a unique human being who is equal and has inalienable rights because she/he is a human being. Some of these inalienable rights include the right to pursue happiness, the right to be a unique individual, the right to think or believe as she/he wishes, the right to pursue his/her life's

yearnings and the right to self-defense. People can be arrested or detained only with direct order from a judge or magistrate who is responsible for the arrest/detention. A person arrested or detained should have the right to immediately notify her/his relatives and friends. Arrest or detention of foreigners should be subject to international law.

(8)   We should look into having a jury system whereby a group of private citizens verify the facts of the offense and the Judge interprets the intent of the law to pass judgment.

(9)   Power of Mercy: Only the Chief Creator upon advice of the Cabinet has the prerogative of extending mercy to anyone.

Chapter V: Political Branches

Please do not dismiss our models: I invite you to come and study our systems. Let us also contribute to the evolution of political thought because I do not like the role of just being a consumer of political ideas: I, too, would like to be a contributor to political thought. (Museveni, pg. 246)

Article 40. General Provisions.

The political branches are called arms of government: the Legislative arm and the Executive arm. The Speaker of Parliament heads the legislature while the President of the Cabinet heads the Executive.

Sub Chapter One: Branch Three-The Legislative Arm

Article 41. General Provisions.

This is the arm of government responsible for

making all specific laws of the country. The Legislative arm of government should be called Parliament and its members should be called Members of Parliament or MPs. Parliament has the authority to remove the President in an impeachment trial, which should take not more than six months but more than four months.

ARTICLE 42. THE PARLIAMENT

(1)   The Parliament is entrusted with enacting all specific laws of the country, even if initiation of laws can be by any citizen. All specific laws have to reference an article of the general law under which they fall. A citizen can contribute to Parliamentary debates with permission from her/his MP. Parliament on its first sitting elects a Speaker and two Deputy Speakers in an election presided over by the Chief Justice. A person can be Speaker up to two parliamentary terms, i.e. up to eight years.

(2)   **Passage of Acts**: The president has to assent to all bills before they become law. If the President refuses

to assent to a bill, it has to go back to parliament for further discussion. Afterwards, it can be resent to the President and if she/he does not assent to it, it returns to the Parliament. If for the third time the President refuses to assent to it, the bill goes to the Supreme Court, which could ascent to the bill.

(3)	If a new specific law leads to a different interpretation of the Constitution, the National Assembly can amend the Constitution with 3 out of 4 votes whereby the measure has to get a 66% support from each approving national branch.

(4)	Due to the expansion of public life to include a fourth branch, parliament should have as few members as possible, preferably between 100 and 271 MPs. Parliamentary elections take place two months before the National Day. Any citizen can be an MP for any area in the country as long as she/he resides there.

(5)	There are select committees that initiate bills

before they are tabled to a full parliamentary debate. There should be an effort to balance the age on committees by having young MPs and older MPs.

ARTICLE 43. THE MEMBERS OF PARLIAMENT (MPs)

(1)   Anyone above 21 years of age who can read and write can be elected on individual merit or under a party. MPs are elected for four-year terms, renewable indefinitely. Half of the MPs are elected every two years. Any MP can be recalled back by his/her constituency in which case a by-election is held within 60 days to replace the former MP. Youth MPs are elected for two years, renewable once.

(2)   There are two types of MPs, Representatives and Special Interest groups. a) Representative MPs – these are elected from national constituencies. One person based on his/her ability rather than tribal affiliation will represent each national constituency. The Electoral commission is

entrusted with dividing or merging Local Councils into numbered constituencies so that there is between 100 and 271 representative MPs who go to parliament. These MPs should be elected by direct popular votes in their constituencies in elections funded by the government with strict guidelines on political party or personal funding. b) Special Interest MPs – these are 30 MPs in five categories: two MPs representing the native Batwa and Bambuti communities, two women MPs from each region, two youth MPs elected by universal suffrage by youths between the ages of 16 and 32 in each region, two MPs of the disabled elected from each region and four MPs each representing a continental region, i.e. Central, Southern, West and North Africa.

(3)   Members of Parliament should meet with their Local Councils on a quarterly basis to coordinate their national duties with local development needs.

ARTICLE 44. MISCELLANEOUS CLAUSES

(1)   The Power of One: Similar to the filibuster procedure, any member of parliament by way of verbal discourse can indefinitely extend debate on any issue as long as the issue does not have 60% support from MPs.

(2)   Government entering into any business contract should require the approval of Parliament.

(3)   In accordance with article 23 (3), Parliament shall not have the power to enact a law establishing a one party state or enact laws of a religious nature (whether indigenous or foreign religion).

Sub Chapter Two: Branch Four -The Executive Arm

ARTICLE 45. GENERAL PROVISIONS.

This is the branch of highest political leadership in the country. The highest executive body in the country is the Cabinet headed by the President who is the Head of Government.

ARTICLE 46. THE HEAD OF GOVERNMENT

(1)   The official title for the head of the cabinet should be " The President of the Cabinet and Head of Government". The duty of the President is to set national policy that guides the cabinet ministers in their managerial roles of working for the betterment of the citizenry. The official home and office for the President should be The Executive Mansion. The minimum qualifications for the presidency should be general enough such that majority of our people can meet them.

(2)   The whole country universally elects the President as stipulated in article 11. The President, together with two Vice Presidents, is elected for a four-year term, renewable only once. Before assuming official state duties, the President-elect swears the *Oath of President (see*

137

appendix). Upon assuming office, the President ceases being an active member of his/her party.

(3)   To prevent an imperial presidency, the President or any cabinet member can be impeached and removed from office any time and he/she can be prosecuted after leaving office. The President or cabinet members can be called up by Parliament to justify every decision they make. To facilitate public participation, the cabinet should find a way to solicit public input about government performance e.g. through online forums and citizen forums.

(4)   Any citizen, born or naturalized, can be elected President. Parliament should decide the maximum age limit for the President, but the minimum age should be the same as for MPs. The main qualification for a president is someone who can govern and make sound decisions in the interest of the state. Political parties can converse votes for a candidate but upon accession to power, the President swears allegiance not to any political party but to the state. The President cannot be an active member of a political

party for the full duration of his/her term. Parliament can remove the President for violation of law or for being unfit, upon which each Vice President becomes President for half the rest of the remaining presidential tenure. In such a situation, the partial term does not count as a first term.

(5)   The President appoints a chief of staff to assist him/her with Executive Mansion business and a Secretary of the Cabinet to help him/her with cabinet business. These two appointees don't need parliamentary confirmation.

(6)   The two Vice Presidents are the official deputies to the President in all matters. Unlike the President, the Vice Presidents can continue being active members of their parties for the duration of their tenure as VPs. They are both elected together with the President. The Vice Presidents take the *Oath of President/Vice President* before assuming office (*see appendix*).

ARTICLE 47. THE CABINET

(1)   The cabinet is made up of 12 ministers (*see section below*) who serve as the administrative/governing body of our country. The only role of cabinet is to improve the standards of living of all citizens by implementing the President's policies. Cabinet ministries are headed by professional non-political managers/administrators. Cabinet members cannot be members of parliament or be active members of political parties. Before assuming office, cabinet members have to say the *Oath of Cabinet* (*see appendix*)

(3)   The president nominates the 12 cabinet ministers who are confirmed by Parliament for a **five-year** term. Since the President is elected for a four-year term, this means each incoming President will find an acting cabinet already in place. At any time upon assuming office, the President has the right to fire any minister and nominate another one. This system will ensure that at each Presidential election, people will be voting for a

new President and new policies but not campaigning for Cabinet positions. Until that time when tribalism does not exist, effort should be made to have a diverse cabinet. Each cabinet member heads a ministry and he/she should address the parliament about specific issues concerning government business at least every quarter.

(4)   Any citizen, born or naturalized, can be appointed to the Cabinet. Parliament should decide the maximum age limit for Cabinet ministers, but the minimum age should be the same as for MPs. The main qualification for a cabinet member is someone who can administer and make sound decisions in the interest of the public. Parliament can remove a cabinet member from office for violation of law or for being unfit, upon which another person is nominated by the President.

(5)   The cabinet should consist of the President and two Vice Presidents, plus the following 12 ministries. Each ministry is further subdivided into departments headed by Permanent Secretaries. Permanent Secretaries are also

appointed by the President and confirmed by parliament for **five-year** terms. In the following list, departments are in parenthesis.

- Finance and Economics (Fiscal Policy, Economic Planning, Microfinance, etc)

- Commerce (Industry, Trade, etc)

- Natural Resources (Water, Minerals, Forestry, Land Management, etc)

- Infrastructure (IT, Transportation, Housing, Urban Development, Public works, etc)

- Energy

- Agriculture, Animal Industry and Fisheries

- Local Government (District Affairs, Local Council Affairs, etc)

- Attorney general (Constitutional affairs, Justice, Solicitor General etc)

- Foreign Affairs (East Africa, Africa, General relations, etc)

- Internal Affairs (Tourism, Security, National Census, Immigration services, etc)

- Social Welfare (Relief and Disaster

preparedness, Labor, Equality, Disability, etc)

- Sustainability (Economic sustainability, Environmental sustainability, etc)

(6) **Cabinet Ranking members**: There are two other cabinet level positions that don't require Parliamentary approval: the Secretary to the Cabinet and the Chief of Staff of the Executive Mansion. These two cabinet members serve four-year terms, just like the President. The President and Vice Presidents do not have specific ministerial duties other than overall cabinet coordination.

(7) **Other Executive Offices**: There should be other executive offices, which function independent of the Cabinet. They are nominated by the President and confirmed by Parliament for five-year terms.

- National AIDS Commissioner
- National Environment Management Agency
- UN Ambassador
- African Union Ambassador

- Children Affairs Commissioner
- The National Gazette

(8) **Presidential Advisors**: These are people appointed by the President, without Parliamentary approval, to offer professional advice and analysis of specific issues. Example of such advisors are: Economic advisers, Science and Technology advisers, indigenous culture advisers, literacy adviser, the Press Secretary, national policy adviser, education adviser, security advisers, climate and environmental adviser, national history adviser, trade and commerce adviser, etc.

CHAPTER VI: INTER-BRANCH OFFICES

ARTICLE 48. GENERAL PROVISIONS.

These are Independent offices set up to offer objective assessment of the four branches of government and take charge of important national tasks that need to be independent of any of the four branches of national authority. They are nominated by the Chief Creator, seconded by the cabinet and confirmed by Parliament for a term of five years, renewable four times. All the offices have their seats in the central region. At any time, Parliament can relieve these office bearers of their duties due to corruption, ineptitude or unethical behavior.

ARTICLE 49. THE NATIONAL ELECTORAL COMMISSION

The commission manages all elections in the country. It manages all national and district elections directly, and all Local Council elections indirectly through District Electoral Boards.

ARTICLE 50. THE AUDITOR GENERAL

The office is to financially audit all branches of public authority (national, district and local). The Auditor General has assistants for each district and local council.

ARTICLE 51. THE INSPECTOR GENERAL OF GOVERNMENT

The duty of the Inspector General of Government [IGG] is to inspect and coordinate the smooth coexistence of two political branches and the two non-political branches of the nation-state together with the 2 levels of local government. The office also evaluates the functioning of all government officials.

ARTICLE 52. NATIONAL BUDGET OFFICE

(1)   This is the office that assesses the budgets of all government entities and also proposes the salaries and benefits for all public officials. Parliament has to approve the office's assessments and recommendations. The office collects inputs from all government entities and officially presents the National budget to the Parliament.

(2)   **Salaries and benefits**: The National Budget Office should draw up a salary and benefits schedule for all the four branches of authority. In descending order, the salaries should be greatest for the Chief Creator, then the Supreme Court, then the Cabinet and lastly the Parliament. However, total benefits should be based on how many engagements, meetings, travels, public functions, etc are carried out by the individual national branch leaders, hence the total benefits will be highest for the Cabinet.

ARTICLE 53. BROADCASTING COMMISSION

The Commission loosely regulates all media in the

country. Government should not own media houses other than the national Gazette.

ARTICLE 54. DIRECTORATE OF PUBLIC PROSECUTIONS

The office's mandate is to work in the interest of the public by prosecuting anyone, whether in government or not, for criminal offenses.

ARTICLE 55. PUBLIC SERVICE COMMISSION

All civil and public servants have to be cleared by the Public Service Commission before they embank on their public duties.

CHAPTER VII: LOCAL GOVERNMENT ADMINISTRATION

ARTICLE 56. GENERAL PROVISIONS.

(1)   The land, air and water of the country should be divided into two-tier local government administrative divisions: the first tier unit should be called Local Councils (Villages, Towns, Municipalities and Cities), and the second tier unit should be districts. Whereas citizens set up Local Council units, the Districts divisions are setup and approved by Parliament. Both Local Councils and Districts don't make laws, but rather they make regulations and ordinances. The National Electoral Commission directly manages district elections, while District Electoral Boards set up by the national commission manage Local

Council elections. The Local Councilors and District Administrators are elected on an individual-merit or national party basis.

(2)   Both Local Councils and Districts are loosely supervised by the national government, specifically the ministry of Local Governance. The National authorities should strictly monitor Local Councils and Districts to ensure that minority people's rights are fundamentally honored and respected. In order to work towards having local governing institutions that do not discriminate against cultural minorities, each person entrusted with local government administration should say the *Oath of Service* (see schedules section at the end) and work to uphold it. The Local Government Ministry appoints a Resident Commissioner for each Local Council and District council. The Resident Commissioner's job is non-political. He/She works as the direct liaison coordinating the national government and the local government.

(3)   Constituencies for national elections should be

based on Local Council demarcations to cut costs on having to make brand new constituents. Several Local Councils might have one MP or within a single Local Councils there could be several MPs.

(4)   There should be four autonomous national Local Councils (operated by the four national branches), one in each region, which should serve as seats for the four branches of national authority.

Sub Chapter One: First Local Government Division

ARTICLE 57. GENERAL PROVISIONS.

(5)   Citizens independently create the first local administrative division called a Local Council. If it is a rural area, it is called a Village Council. If it is an urban area, it is either a Town Council, Municipal Council or City Council. The Local Government Ministry makes the urban/rural demarcations. Local Councils are the smallest national political units.

(6)   For each Local Council internal administration, village councils will be called Counties (emisaza), which can further sub divide themselves in to sub-counties (gombolola), and urban areas can sub divide themselves into parishes (emiluka). The two sub-divisions don't have political significance but rather they are entities created to organize within the Local Councils.

(7)   Local Councils are the power retaining units of the political state and all government effort should be geared towards making sure they function efficiently. Local Councils are divisions that will allow greater flexibility and ingenuity by citizens to manage their own affairs and also allow greater localization of the essential aspects of life. The national and district institutions of government are there to guide Local Councils in their role of bettering the citizenry.

(8)   The citizens elect the Local Councils according to guidelines set up by the respective District Electoral Boards. Local Councils should be made up of councilors

representing each sub-division and a mayor who performs the executive duties. The councilors perform the legislative duty of making regulations and ordinances. The Mayor is the executive head. The mayor is universally elected for a term of three years renewable twice. There are two Vice Mayors.

(9) The Local Council Police Chief is nominated by the District Police Chief and confirmed by the Local Council.

Sub Chapter Two: Second Local Government Division

ARTICLE 58. GENERAL PROVISIONS.

(1) Parliament should permanently set up the demarcations for the second local government division called Districts. Parliament should group rural and urban local councils into a unit called a district. We should work to revert the number of districts to the original 19 districts, or if there is plausible reason to split these 19 original

districts, it should not exceed 36 districts. Districts cannot be based on tribal identity. For example, instead of having a district for the Basoga called Busoga, we should use the formula of bundling both rural and urban Local Councils into a district that we could give the name of the major town (this was the formula used to create the original districts of Jinja, Iganga, and Kamuli). To prevent people yearning to carve out numerous districts, the people should be reminded that the real political power is at the Local Council level, not at the district level. Districts are a mere coordinating entity between Local Councils and the National government.

(2)   No district can be formed on a tribal basis because this theoretically leads to 56 district entities (the current number of tribes in the country) and because of inter-tribal migrations, such an ethnic based nation is logically and practically impossible to build. Even if some district might naturally have one "indigenous" tribe, government should strictly ensure that district business is carried out based on non-tribal basis. All tribal aspirations are purely

cultural, not political or economical and they should be channeled to the Chwezia Librarian's office.

(3)   Districts should be purely administrative units between Local Councils and the national government. The present debate of whether our country should be federal or unitary is irrelevant as long as the nation agrees on this creative alternative model of governance. As discussed in the four branches sections, this republican proposal is a creative hybrid system of governance. The government will not be a traditional federal type because instead of the regions or districts being represented in parliament, we shall have the population represented in Parliament while cultural interests are represented in the Heritage branch via the Chwezi Librarian. I strongly believe this is a genuinely original idea that fits well with the realities of our tribal heritages but also meets the demands of a modern state. We have to be creative to form a national structure that checks and avoids any potential tribal conflicts. Also, the government will not be a traditional unitary type, because all local and district administrators will be universally

elected with no influence from the central government. No district or local council can restrict settlement of people from other regions, and trade cannot be restricted across district or local council lines.

(4)   Districts will have only an executive arm, which refers to Local Council ordinances and national laws to carry out its administrative roles. The District Administrator [DA] and Assistant DAs are the executive committee that leads each District Administration. The DA is universally elected for a three-year term, renewable twice. The Assistant DAs are elected by their respective Local Councils for a three-year term renewable indefinitely. The District Administration should be at the District Headquarters. The DA should communicate to district residents on a weekly basis.

(5)   Districts have power to administer people, supervise local administrative units and perform any other duty assigned by the cabinet or parliament. Districts should supervise their local councils in the running of the

emergency services like fire departments and disaster response teams.

(6)   The District police chief is nominated by the National Police and confirmed by the District Administration.

(7)   The Cabinet should have the power to dissolve District Administration and also veto any ordinance or regulation by the local councils.

CHAPTER VIII: WHAT NEXT?

ARTICLE 59. GENERAL PROVISIONS.

(1)   Personally, I am going to use the profits from the sale of this book to play my part in this general vision. I will play my part in two ways: 1) the building of a library in Iganga town (see conceptual design at the end of this book), which I hope in the future will be incorporated in the National Chwezi Library system, and 2) I am going to find opportunities to give financial aid to poor Ugandans who want to publish their own books so that we each embark on the literacy campaign talked about in this book.

(2)   If this new model of our republic does not bring

about consensus concerning how to go forward in building our nation anew, it must be rejected or ignored. But if it has ideas that can bring about consensus, it should be accepted and promulgated with the necessary modifications. It is my strong belief that at anytime in the future, one of our 31 million citizens will come up with a more perfect model for the fourth republic or better yet, one will come up with a model for a fifth republic. Hence, since the ideas in this model are not set in stone, national parliament should encourage and be on the look-out for any improvements that citizens might bring forth concerning how our country should be structured.

(3)   An alternative to adopting the ideas in this Fourth Republic model is to use this model in the structuring of the proposed East African Federation. The following is my brief framework of how the model of the Fourth Republic can be utilized at the East African Level.

ARTICLE 60. TOWARDS AN EAST AFRICAN REPUBLIC

The five presidents of East Africa have agreed that we should federate into one country some time in the near future. The details of the structure of the federation are still being worked out. The federation as proposed would consist of five provinces: Burundi, Kenya, Rwanda, Tanzania and Uganda.

1. The federation should be called a name that has indigenous significance; I propose the name Chwezia because of the reason I gave in the introductory section of this book.

2. The federal authority should be divided into four branches: the first branch of which is the Human Heritage Branch. This branch should have three entities: the Chief Creator, the Creators' Quorum and the Academy of Human Knowledge. All three entities can meet in the Human Heritage Building

(*see chapter 4*). Any tribal language can be used in official Heritage Branch business as long as there is interpretation into the three official federal languages i.e. English, French and Swahili.

3. We should look into two options for a Federal Capital. One option is for the Federal Capital to remain Arusha. The second option is to spread the federal branch seats in four towns in four different regions. For this option, there is need to first demarcate the four regions that could be used.

4. The head of state of the federal republic should be the head of the human heritage branch, namely The Chief Creator.

   a. The Chief Creator is elected similar to how I outlined in Chapter 4.

      i. The Chief Creator has two deputies.

   b. The first arm of the Heritage Branch should be called the Creators' Quorum.

      i. Members are nominated by the Chief Creator,

seconded by the Cabinet and confirmed for life by the Parliament. Creators have no national duties.

ii. The qualification for members is that they have created something that is beneficial to all humanity.

c. The second arm of the human heritage branch should be called "The Chwezi Academy of Human Knowledge".

i. The composition of this body should be as outlined in the main section of the book.

ii. There should also be a federal Librarian concerned with evolving our oral tribal cultures into literary cultures.

5. The second branch of federal authority should be the Judiciary Branch. The head body should be called the Supreme Court.

a. The Chief Creator nominates the Justices of the court who are seconded by the Cabinet and then confirmed by Parliament for a term longer than 2 presidential terms, renewable once.

163

6. The third branch of federal authority is the Legislative Branch represented by a two chamber Parliament (Bunge)

    a. The upper chamber could be called "The Senate".

        i If it is called Senate, each of the current five countries elects three senators for a term of 6 years renewable twice. Every two years, a third of the senators are elected.

    b. The lower chamber of parliament could be called the House of the People

        i. Members can be called MPs and they are chosen from their respective constituencies for a term of 4 years renewable indefinitely.

        ii. The House should have between 200 and 300 members.

        iii. We should consider having some special interest MPs: e.g. youth Mps, women MPs, Disabled MPs and MPs representing the other 4 regions of Africa.

7. The fourth federal branch should be the Executive Branch led by the President of the Cabinet.

a. The president is elected for a term of four years renewable only once.

b. The president has two Vice Presidents and names a cabinet with Senate approval.

c. Cabinet members are appointed for 5-year terms and they cannot be Members of Parliament.

8. There should be a two-tier system for local government administration: Local Councils and the five Provinces.

   a. The Local Councils should remain the three urban councils (Town, Municipals and Cities) and the Village Councils called County Councils.

      i. Local Councils don't make laws, but rather regulations and ordinances.

   b The Provinces (mkoa) should be the five countries

      i. Each province could have an executive branch led by a Governor and a legislative branch represented by a Provincial Council. Members of the Council should be called Councilors to aid with tribal references.

ODE TO THE YOUNG

Ode to the young, creators!

When the world was dull, they created music

Mozart, Beethoven, MJ, Lutaaya, in their teens

When the world was flat, they showed the true nature

Newton, Darwin, Einstein, Heisenberg, in their 20s

When drums were used to communicate, they created computers

Gates, Mark, Dell, Google guys, in their 20s

While society stood static, they pushed

Joan of Arc, one teenage girl

King and Lumumba, mere 26

Washington, Jefferson, Mandela, 33

Jesus of Nazareth, son of man, 30

Ode to the young, creators!

Ode to the young, YOU!

Schedules

Schedule 1: The first Ugandan Flag

Between March and October 1962, this was the Ugandan national flag.

Source: http://flagspot.net/flags/ug.html)

Schedule 2: UPC Historical Flag

This is the UPC party flag that was later adopted as the national flag.

Source: http://flagspot.net/flags/ug.html

Schedule 3a: The National Anthem "Oh Uganda"

Red stanza.

Oh Uganda! May God uphold thee;

We lay our future in thy hand.

United, free,

For liberty

Together we'll always stand.

Blue stanza.

Oh Uganda! The land of freedom.

Our love and labour we give,

And with neighbours all

At our country's call

In peace and friendship we'll live.

Yellow stanza.

Oh Uganda! The land that feeds us

By sun and fertile soil grown.

For our own dear land,

We'll always stand:

The Pearl of Africa's Crown

SCHEDULE 3B: UGANDA SCHOOL ANTHEM

Chorus.

We young women and men of Uganda

Are marching along the path of education

Singing and Dancing with joy together

Uniting for a better Uganda

Verse 1.

We are the pillar of tomorrow's Uganda

Let us rise now embrace true knowledge

Yielding disciplined resourcefulness

To rebuild a great, great pearl

Verse 2.

We know the way into the land of enlightenment

Has thorns, creepers, vales, and mountains

Come what may we shall overcome

For the glorious times to come

Verse 3.

Parents and teachers and the youths of this nation

Rise with us, support our endeavors

Led by God who is the Source of Life

To uplift our motherland

SCHEDULE 4: PROPOSED FLAG TO MATCH THE NATIONAL ANTHEM

(Blue and Yellow have been interchanged for better contrast)

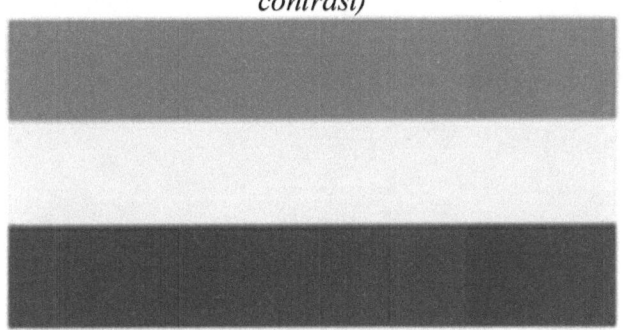

SCHEDULE 5: OATHS OF OFFICE

Oath of Allegiance

I, _____ pledge allegiance to the Republic of Chwezia, one nation, indivisible in its diversity. I pledge to upload the values that the nation stands for. Within the laws and institutions of the republic, I will play my part in creating a better world for all. I pledge to develop my independence of thought and educate myself so I can contribute to the Pearl of African's Crown. For

God and my Country.

The current Oath of Allegiance:

I_____, swear in the name of the Almighty God/ solemnly affirm that I will be faithful and bear true allegiance to the Republic of Uganda and that I will preserve, protect and defend the Constitution. [So help me God.]

Oath of Redemption

I, _____ do solemnly request that the people of Chwezia forgive me for the crimes of _____, _____, _____ that I have rendered upon the common humanity of our peoples. I acknowledge that some people rightfully think I don't deserve redemption, but I am an imperfect human being just like every one of us. I pledge to live within the laws of the republic from hereon. I will learn, serve and work for the betterment of all peoples. For God and My Country.

Oath of Chief Creator/Deputy Chief Creator

I, _____ do solemnly affirm that

I will truthfully exercise the function of Chief Creator/ Deputy Chief Creator to the best of my ability. I will serve the nation without partiality so that my work can promote the welfare not only of the citizens of the Republic but all of humanity. Fellow Chwezians, with your trust and confidence, I will lead, guide and defend the ideas of the Chwezi Republic. For God and My Country.

Oath of Human Heritage

I, _____ do solemnly affirm that I will faithfully continue to be an example in showcasing the creative spirit in each of us. I will serve the nation and all of humanity by _____. I will do this For God and My Country.

Oath of the Judiciary

I, _____ do solemnly affirm that I will truthfully exercise the function of the office of _____ according to the laws of the Republic. I will serve all citizens without fear or favor, affection or ill will. I pledge to use my critical faculties and develop my independence of thought so that I can make my own judgment to provide justice to all citizens under the guidance of our human heritage laws. Fellow Chwezians, with your trust and confidence, I will uphold universal justice. For God and my Country.

The current Judicial Oath:

I_____, swear in the name of the Almighty, God/ solemnly affirm that I will well and truly exercise the judicial functions entrusted to me and will do right to all manner of people in accordance with the Constitution of the Republic of Uganda as by law established and in accordance with the laws and usage of the Republic of Uganda without fear or favour, affection or ill will. [So help me God.]

Oath of the Legislature

I, _____ do solemnly affirm that I will be truthful to my conscience and exercise the national duty of representing the people of _____ in the august Parliament of the republic. I solemnly affirm that my representation will check and balance the workings of the Cabinet. I pledge to work for the welfare not only of my [tribe, religion or] constituents but for all the citizens of the Republic. For God and My Country.

The current Oath of Member of Parliament:

I_____, swear in the name of the Almighty, God/ solemnly affirm that I will give faithful service to this Parliament and support and uphold the Constitution of the Republic of Uganda as by law established. [So help me God.]

Oath of President/ Vice-President

I, _____ do solemnly affirm that I will truthful exercise the function of the office of the President/Vice President of the Republic. I pledge to use my critical faculties and develop my independence of thought to work for the betterment of all citizens. I pledge to uphold, preserve and protect all the laws of the Republic and to promote the welfare of all citizens. Fellow Chwezians, with your trust and confidence, I will lead, guide and defend the republic. For God and My Country.

The current Oath of President/Vice President:

I_____, swear in the name of the Almighty, God/ solemnly affirm that I shall faithfully exercise the function of the President/Vice President of Uganda and shall uphold, preserve and defend the Constitution and observe the laws of Uganda and that I shall promote the welfare of the people of Uganda. [So help me God]

Oath of Cabinet

I, _____ do solemnly swear that I will truthful exercise the function of the office of _____. I pledge to use my critical faculties and develop my independence of thought to work for the betterment of all citizens. I pledge to uphold, preserve and protect all the laws of the Republic and to promote the welfare of all citizens. Fellow Chwezians, with your trust and confidence, I will work For God and My Country.

The current Oath of Minister:

I_____, being appointed a Minister of Uganda swear

in the name of the Almighty, God/solemnly affirm that

I will at all times well and truly server the Republic

of Uganda in the office of a Minster; and that I will

support and uphold the Constitution of the Republic of

Uganda as by law established; and that I will to the best

of my judgment at all times when required, freely give

my counsel and advice to the President of Uganda and

his/her successors in office as by law established for the

good management of the public affairs of the Republic

of Uganda; and that I will not directly or indirectly

reveal any matter as shall come to my knowledge in the

discharge of my duties and committed to my secrecy.

[So help me God]

Oath of Service

I, _____ solemnly affirm that

I will fairly and justly serve all individuals living in

_____ without prejudice, segregation, or malice.

I pledge to respect the humanity in each individual and

make decisions in line with my conscience under the guidelines of our Human Heritage ideals. I will do this so that my work will benefit everyone irrespective of tribe, religion or area of origin. For God and my Country.

GLOSSARY

Academy of human knowledge: The second arm of the Heritage Branch of the Fourth republic

Chief Creator: The head of the Heritage Branch of the Fourth Republic, who also acts as the head of state of the country.

Chwezi Creator: A member of the Creators' Quorum. A citizen offered national honor for service to humanity by excelling in a creative personal endeavor.

Chwezi Creators' Quorum: One of the two arms of the Heritage Branch of the Fourth Republic, which comprises individuals that have created things for the benefit of all humanity.

Generation: 30 earth years

Human Heritage Republic: the type of nation-state that

the Fourth Heritage stands for. A country in which every person's human heritage is represented in the Human Heritage branch.

National Assembly: An annual summit at which all four branches of the nation meet.

National Day: The first day of our year, also a public holiday in which we celebrate our nationhood and human heritage.

Movement: An organization formed by citizens to fundamentally change the system of the country.

Republic Vote: A nationwide election for the purpose of changing the constitution, changing the nature of the republic or electing the Chief Creator, in which the general population has four votes, and each of the four branches of state has one vote. For an issue to pass the vote, it requires seven out of the eight votes.

State Assembly: A semi-annual summit for the cabinet, parliament and district administrators

References

1. Bronowski, Jacob. The Ascent of Man: A Personal View by J. Bronowski. Ambrose Video Publishing, Inc. (2006)

2. Flags of the World Website. http://flagspot.net/flags/ug.html (May 21, 2009)

3. Mazrui, Ali, A. The Africans: A Triple Heritage. Little Brown And Company, Boston (1986).

4. Museveni, Yoweri, K. What is Africa's Problem? University of Minnesota Press, Minneapolis (2000).

5. Nzita, Richard and Mbaga-Niwampa. Peoples and Cultures of Uganda. Kampala: Fountain Publishers Ltd., 1997.

6.   Webster's Ninth New Collegiate Dictionary. Springfield. Merriam-Webster Inc. (1983)

7.   Woolman, Michael. <u>Ways of Knowing: An Introduction to Theory of Knowledge</u> Victoria, IBID Press (2000).

THE IGANGA LIBRARY

All profits from the sale of this book will be used in two ways: 1) the building of a library in Iganga town (see conceptual plan below), and 2) giving financial aid to poor Ugandans who want to publish their own books.

Figure 8: Conceptual Iganga Library

ABOUT THE AUTHOR

Mr. Kirunda was born in Iganga Town in 1979 to Mr. Sanoni Atanaziraba and Ms. Edinansi Nakisita. This is the continuation book for his first book *The Fourth Heritage* in which he wrote about the mental roadmap for integrating our triple heritages of tribe, religion and colonial heritages.

Since both his parents were illiterate, in both his books, the author is trying to write from the point view of illiterate tribal people like his parents who have no voice in the current debates about our society.

He attended Iganga Town Council Primary School (1986 –1989) and Nkumba Primary School (1990 –1993). In 1994 Mr. Kirunda started his secondary school at King's College Budo. After senior four, Budo nominated him for the United World College scholarship national contest, at which he was selected to go represent Uganda at the United World College-USA. He is eternally grateful to the then Budo Headmaster, Mr. Sam Busuulwa who gave him a list of 20 prominent Bodonians from whom he was able to fundraise money for his upkeep in the USA. He did his Bachelor's in Engineering at Lafayette College (Pennslyvania) and Master of Science in Engineering at the University of Texas at Austin. After working five years as a Civil Engineer in New Mexico and Texas, he currently works in the Investment Banking industry in Salt Lake City, Utah. In his leisure time, Mr. Kirunda enjoys playing rugby, skiing, biking, running, swimming and exploring the beautiful American Southwest region.